The Annual Monitor and Memorandum Book (Or, Obituary of the Members of the Society of Friends). 1813-19 All of the 2Nd Ed. as Vol. 1 With a General Title-Leaf and Index 1813-32, 22, 33-37, 39; 43 - 1919-20
by Society of Friends

Address:
HardPress
8345 NW 66TH ST #2561
MIAMI FL 33166-2626
USA
Email: info@hardpress.net

ANNUAL
MONITOR
1871.

Per. 11141 f. 5

New Series, No. 29.

THE

ANNUAL MONITOR

For 1871,

OR

OBITUARY

OF THE

MEMBERS OF THE SOCIETY OF FRIENDS

In Great Britain and Ireland,

FOR THE YEAR 1870.

LONDON:

SOLD BY F. B. KITTO AND E. MARSH.

WILLIAM SESSIONS, 15, LOW OUSEGATE, YORK.

THOMAS EDMONDSON, 11, DAME STREET, DUBLIN.

1870.

NAMES WITH MEMOIRS.

Susannah H. Barrow.
Henry Bowman.
Edward Brewin.
Elizabeth Candler.
Joseph Cash.
Joseph Doubleday.
Eliza H. Gregory.
Maria Jacob.
Grover Kemp.
Sarah Littleboy.
Mary Ann Luscombe.
Samuel Marshall.
Henry Moorhouse.
Mary Mounsey.
Sophia Pease.
Thomas Rathbone.

Thomas Sharpe.
Maria Simms.
Elizabeth Southall.
Jacob Sparrow.
William Thistlethwaite.
George Thomas.
Sarah Thompson.
Richd. Wm. Thompson.
Edwin Thompson, M.B.
Sarah Wadham.
Sarah Wakeford.
Marion Webb.
Mary Wigham, *Carlisle*.

———

Josiah Forster.

APPENDIX.

Eliza Lockwood.
Joseph Benwell.

———

Errata in the last Volume, 1870.

At page 72—For *Margaret*, read *Mary* Evens.
———— 169—For *James*, read *Jane* Stephens.
———— 169—For Albert and John *Stule*, read *Steele*.
———— 100—For *Daughter* of John Heppenstall,
read *Widow*. N.B. H. H. was a daughter of
Thos. Shillitoe.

PREFACE.

Glancing over the names of those whose memorials occupy a place in this volume, we find a great variety of character and experience. Some seem to have outlived their generation, and only few remain who knew them in the vigour of their day. It may be both useful and refreshing to look back at their career, and recall their services. With advancing years, they withdrew from the field of labour,—not unmindful of the harvest or the labourers, but watching and waiting for the call to "enter into the joy of their Lord." Others were setting out, as it might be thought, on a career full of promise —being early made sensible, through the visitations of the Holy Spirit, of the exceeding love of God in Christ. They were entering the ranks of the Lord's army, they began to run well, and we had fondly hoped they would advance in knowledge and in grace,—when lo! they are suddenly removed : we grieve over their departure, but all we can say is, Thy will be done !

It is the Almighty's prerogative to appoint to all their places, and it is our part to look out for the work He ordains for us, with ready and willing hearts. Often does the enlightened mind, when made conscious that the end is near, feel that if life on earth could again be renewed, it would have to be spent differently, and more devoted to Him who gave it. Yet there are not wanting those who, watchfully and diligently following their Lord and Master, are strengthened in every conflict, and enjoy that perfect peace with God through Christ, that renders life not only useful but happy, and death welcome as a messenger of joy unspeakable.

"See in what peace a Christian can die!" It is encouraging to find this truth afresh illustrated from year to year in our simple pages. The stroke may be sudden or even instantaneous, but there is no ground for fear; or the close may be in view for months, but the promises are sure. Even a child may grasp them. The youthful disciple, to whom the hopes of this life are unfolding, is enabled to realize that "to depart and be with Christ is far better:"—and the weary pilgrim, or the veteran in the Lord's service, is cheered with the prospect of entering into rest. We rejoice in the belief that so many of our Friends, including those of whom we have no especial record, have left behind them evidence, that they did expire in peace, and in the assurance of a blessed immortality.

But is it not possible there may be names in this registry of some, whose departure was shrouded in uncertainty?—a mist hanging impenetrable over the unseen world to come! We tremble at the thought. We dare not follow such to the great tribunal, saying "How shall they appear?" Rather let our questioning come home to our own hearts:—"For *we must all appear* before the judgment seat of Christ, that every one may receive the things done in his body, according to that he hath done, whether it be good or bad:" (2 Cor. v. 10). And how shall *we* appear? Where is our advocate? Where is our pardon? Where is our refuge? If these are awful inquiries, they are needful, they are urgent. We cannot alter the sentence: "Every one of us shall give account of himself to God." But we have an advocate with the Father, —we have a place of refuge, if only we do not neglect to flee to it. "God hath not appointed us to wrath, but to obtain salvation through our Lord Jesus Christ." Let us make sure of this prize. If we give up our hearts to God, believing on the Lord Jesus, the Holy Spirit is shed upon us abundantly through Him, our sins are washed out, we are born again, the things done in our body are wrought in Christ, and we inherit everlasting life. Glorious consummation! and yet, in Infinite mercy, placed within the reach of all.

But while these reflections arise on the removal of three hundred of our Friends during the past twelve months, with what harrowing thoughts do we turn to the thousands upon thousands, who in as many weeks have descended into battle and perished!—slain by their fellow-men, and by so-called fellow-Christians! Is the voice addressed to the first slayer no longer audible? "What hast thou done? The voice of thy brother's blood crieth to me from the ground." Here are streams of our brothers' blood! graves numberless! a country wasted! cities destroyed! a nation famished! Rare indeed is the earthquake, hurricane or storm, that in its devastating track equals this devastation. Well might the King of Israel say, "Let me now fall into the hands of the Lord, for His mercies are great,—but let me not fall into the hands of men!"

Whilst our hearts bleed over the woes of our suffering fellow-creatures,—whilst we mourn over the name of Christ dishonoured and His kingdom and government rejected amongst the nations,—let us be doubly careful to bear a Christian testimony to the peaceful character of His kingdom, and to maintain a true allegiance to Him as the Prince of Peace, who equally rejected the defence of the sword, and the succour of "twelve legions of angels."

JOHN NEWBY.

Ackworth, Twelfth Month, 1870.

THE
ANNUAL MONITOR.
1871.

OBITUARY.

	Age.	Time of Decease.
PAUL ABBATT,	4¼	22 5 mo. 1870
Bolton. Son of William and Ann Abbatt.		
WILLIAM ABBOTT,	82	17 3 mo. 1870
Glanmire, County Cork.		
MARY AIREY,	64	25 10 mo. 1869
Hornicop, near Kendal.		
SARAH AIREY,	69	20 1 mo. 1870
Stoke Newington, London.		
MARY ANNE ALLEN,	57	24 2 mo. 1870
Dundrum, Dublin. Wife of Joseph Allen.		
PETER ALLEY, *Manchester.*	22	31 3 mo. 1870
Son of Peter B. and Catherine Alley.		

THOMAS HENRY ALLIS,   53   1   8 mo. 1870
    Osbaldwick, York.   Son of Thomas and Sarah
    Allis.

JOSEPH ALLISON,   25 11   1 mo. 1870
    Cotherstone.   Son of John and Eleanor Allison.

MATILDA ARMISTEAD,   62 26   5 mo. 1870
    Reigate.

WILLIAM HENRY ASHFORD,   4 25   6 mo. 1870
    Birmingham. Son of William and Ellen Ashford.

ELIZABETH ASHMAN,   86 22   2 mo. 1870
    Yoakley's Buildings, Stoke Newington.

THOMAS ASHWORTH, *Bath.*   67 30   4 mo. 1870

JANE ATKINSON,   57 30   9 mo. 1870
    Lancaster.   Widow of Thomas Atkinson.

JOHN BAKER, *Bristol.*   76 20 11 mo. 1869

DAVID NAINBY BALLANS,   68 22   9 mo. 1870
    Norwich.

HULDAH ISABEL BARRINGTON,
    Bray.   16 28   1 mo. 1870
  Daughter of Edward and Huldah Barrington.

SUSANNA HORNE BARROW,   40 21   5 mo. 1869
    Birmingham.   Wife of George Barrow.

     The name of this Friend appeared in our
Obituary last year. She was the daughter of
Grover and Susannah Kemp, of Brighton, of the
former of whom a record will be found in this
volume.

In her early childhood she was very delicate; and, being the youngest sister in the family, was a source of much care and interest, and her gentle and loving manners greatly endeared her to all the home circle. She became after some years more robust, and subsequently enjoyed a considerable share of health. After her 18th year she entered with warmth and energy into philanthropic objects, the subject of temperance claiming her especial attention.

In the year 1852 she commenced noting her religious feelings in private memoranda; and it is observed from her diary, that whilst on a visit to her brother and sister who resided at Norwich, she derived much spiritual help and instruction from the ministry of our late dear friend William Forster, and that she renewedly felt the blessedness of a surrender of heart to her gracious Saviour. The simplicity of her faith, her love to Jesus, and her devotedness to His cause, are evinced in her memoranda, from which a few extracts will be given; and while they manifest a deeper religious life, than from her reticence on these subjects was known at the time to those by whom she was surrounded, yet was there *then* discernible those precious fruits of the Spirit, only to be derived from union with the true and living Vine.

Eighth month, 19th, 1852. "Have faith in thy Father in Heaven, O my soul; press forward in the narrow way, which only leadeth to the Kingdom of rest and peace. Oh! can I be forgiven? Can my many sins be blotted out? They can, I know, only by the blood of Jesus, and He will not cast out any who come to Him. He is over all, God blessed for ever. Amen."

Sixth month, 1st, 1853. "Have had the great pleasure and privilege of attending the Yearly Meeting; and if I am not deceiving myself, and I trust I am not, I do earnestly desire that I may profit thereby. I feel that I am very frail and weak, and it is delightful to hear tell of the glories of the heavenly kingdom,—of the way being, to the humble and obedient, although the way of the cross, a way of pleasantness, and a path of peace. But when I come to my dear home, surrounded by unnumbered mercies and benefits, I feel too often cold and deadened: and I am too often cast down, not from a right cause, but from an unthankful heart; yet do I long to feel my Saviour near to me every hour, and to glorify Him in all my ways, wherever I am, whoever I am with. He is very precious to me as my Advocate with the Father. I must ever-lastingly have perished, were it not that God was manifest in the flesh, and offered His most precious life a sacrifice for my sins."

Eleventh month, 26th, 1853. "We are much in care sometimes about perplexing earthly things; and it is very strengthening and sweet at such times to leave these things, and endeavour, as ability may be graciously afforded, to look to Jesus. Oh! I have felt a little of the love of my Saviour, at times, drawing me to Himself;—may I cast myself on Him, and commit myself and *all* I love, into His holy hands for time and for eternity! I am persuaded that the true Christian is happier than the worldly-minded man, even in this life; and has the blessed hope of a happy eternity, if he continues to follow Him, who died for him and rose again, and ever liveth to make intercession for poor sinners."

Eighth month, 27th, 1854. "I wrote last time *(at the end of the previous month)* in great distress and conflict of spirit; but I may acknowledge that afterwards while sitting in silence, with earnest desires for forgiveness and help, I found these words brought to me somewhat suddenly and powerfully, "I have blotted out as a cloud thy transgressions, and as a thick cloud thy sins;" accompanied with the belief that all things would eventually be permitted to work for my good.

Oh the peace and calm I felt, so that I only
desired to remain under the blessed feeling of
that love, which seemed to have forgiven me, and
permitted me to feel its sweet trustful influences."

Ninth month, 3rd, 1854. "This year is
rapidly passing away, and another day of rest is
come. I feel somewhat painfully how little I am
doing for the good of my fellow creatures, and
would ask whether something more may not be
required at my hands. O dearest Father, show
me what I must do, if it be Thy holy will, and
give me strength to do it in meekness and fear,
and teach me what to leave undone.—I often feel
low in spirits, and inclined mentally to repeat
these lines,

> 'Hide me—oh my Saviour! hide,
> Till the storm of life be passed,
> Safe into the Haven guide,—
> Oh receive my soul at last!' "

In the year 1855, she was united in marriage
to George Barrow, and became a member of
Birmingham meeting, where she was introduced
into a large circle of relatives and friends, by
whom she was much beloved. The maturity of
her character was conspicuous, and her thoughtful
endeavour rightly to fulfil every duty in her
new station was often apparent, affording a silent,

yet teaching lesson to those with whom she was associated.

Her health seriously gave way in 1861, and she continued with some intervals of renewed vigour, a frequent invalid during the remainder of her life. But though often much confined to the house, she was ever bright and cheerful, evincing much Christian resignation and serenity. It may be truly said, that she carried out the injunction of our blessed Redeemer, " Thou, when thou fastest, anoint thine head, and wash thy face, that thou appear not unto men to fast."

At the close of the year she writes:—" Twelfth month, 31st, 1861. This has been a memorable year to me. I have passed through a little of the ' deep waters,' and faith has been at times very low, under physical weakness, and other causes tending to depress, especially the fear, that through unwatchfulness I had not the sense, as I could wish, and had experienced, of the love and presence in my heart of my precious Saviour: but lately, in unutterable mercy, He appears to have lifted up the light of His countenance upon me, blessed be His name; and in returning health, I feel at times reverently prostrated in gratitude before my heavenly Father for His great mercies, spiritual and temporal. ' Bless the Lord, oh my soul, and all that is within me, bless His holy name.'"

Sixth month, 15th, 1862. "When I feel the cords of the Almighty's love around me, may I give Him thanks, and when clouds intercept the shining of His spirit, may I trust,—trust all, trust ever, trust in the dark, casting all my care on Jesus! May I come frequently and earnestly to the fountain of living water! May I know the voice of the Shepherd, and distinguish it from the voice of the Stranger! For Thy loving-kindness and tender mercy all my life long, I desire, O Lord, to return Thee thanks, and to renew my covenant with Thee. I am very weak, help, Lord, or I perish. And oh! gracious Father, should it please Thee again to restore me to health and strength, may I very earnestly desire to work in Thy vineyard in the way *Thou* shalt appoint! and if not able to do so much as others, may I be found doing the work, for which Thou givest ability, in the daytime!"

In allusion to her appointment of overseer in Birmingham meeting, she writes :—Seventh month, 29th, 1866. "My soul feels cast down, with but little ability to lay hold on the 'great and precious promises' of the gospel ; and yet I have so many mercies, that it seems to me like ingratitude not to *rejoice*, but this is perhaps not always at our command.   Oh for more faith, firm and unwavering, in Him who is the life, the truth and the way !   I feel that my friends esteem me more than they should : and tremble lest my standing in the church militant may be higher, than my station in the school of Christ permits. What can I do, but flee for refuge to the Hope set before me ? go to Jesus as a penitent sinner, with the unfaltering faith of a little child, and say, ' If Thou wilt, thou canst make me clean.' "

Early in the year 1869, her friends painfully observed that her strength was declining, and that her tarriance here was very uncertain, and to this she alluded in a conversation with her beloved husband.

A short time after, in a note to her mother, in allusion to herself and her own prospects, she quoted the words of the hymn :—

> " Lord, I believe thou hast prepared,
>   Unworthy though I be,
>   For me, a blood-bought, free reward,
>   A golden harp for me : "—

and added, " I can live on that blessed assurance."

On the 15th of Fifth month, her dear father was with her, and said, " I hope we shall meet in heaven," when the dear invalid replied,

"Perhaps it will not be long first," as though anticipating that this beloved parent would soon follow her, though he was then in his usual health.

One day she wrote on a slate, which she used in consequence of the weakness of her voice, "I cannot speak much to you, but we must say, 'Not my will, but Thine be done.'" She quietly departed on the evening of the 21st of Fifth month, to be, her friends believe, for ever with that Saviour whom she had known and loved.

MARTHA BASS,   74   5 11 mo. 1869
  Feering Lodge, Kelvedon. Widow of William Bass, of Sudbury. Not a recorded Minister, but her communications in our meetings were truly acceptable.

WILLIAM BEAUMONT,   79   9 11 mo. 1869
  Newcastle upon Tyne.

JOHN BELL,   88 21 12 mo. 1869
  Lower Grange, County Antrim.

THOMAS BERRY,   89 19   2 mo. 1870
  Whitechapel, London.

WILLIAM BLAIN, *Waterford.* 73   8   1 mo. 1870

ELIZABETH BOADLE,   32 13   9 mo. 1870
  Birkenhead. Daughter of Mary Boadle and William deceased.

MARTHA BOLTON,   89 28   3 mo. 1870
  Rochdale. Widow of James Bolton.

MARY BOLTON,   61   1   6 mo. 1870
  Penketh, near Warrington.
PRISCILLA BOTT,   81 28   4 mo. 1870
  Hatfield Peverel.   Widow of William Bott.
ARCHIBALD BOUCHER,   82 23   2 mo. 1870
  Sea Park, near Belfast.
KATHARINE ELIZABETH BOWLY,
  Cirencester.   30 14   6 mo. 1870
  Wife of Christopher Bowly.
HENRY BOWMAN,   76   2   8 mo. 1870
  *The Elms, Ashford, near Bakewell, late of One
  Ash Grange.*   An Elder.

This deservedly beloved Friend had been
suffering more or less from a slight paralytic
attack for some months, when he was suddenly
called away. The attitude in which he was found,
and the sweet serenity of his countenance, indi-
cated that the vital spark had fled without conflict. He had risen that morning in more than
usual vigour; and while at breakfast remarked,
that if he felt as well in another month, he hoped
to be at the Quarterly meeting at Nottingham.
Breakfast being over, he read impressively the
20th chapter of the Acts; several verses of which
seemed remarkably applicable to his life, and
final separation from his family and friends.
Soon after the reading he left the room, to be seen

alive no more.   How vividly, on the discovery of
their loss, were his family reminded of the concluding words of that memorable chapter, which
had rested on the minds of more than one with
unusual impressivness, from the moment of their
utterance !

For nine years Henry Bowman was a member of the Committee of Ackworth School, and
notwithstanding that he usually had to drive the
distance of forty-five miles each way, he was very
regular in his attendance.   He also for many
years filled the important stations of overseer and
elder in his own meeting ; and occasionally, in
obedience to what he believed to be required of
him, his voice was heard in meetings for worship,
to the comfort and help of the few who usually
met with him.

The more enlarged views of Gospel labour
entertained by our Religious Society at first
induced a feeling of anxiety ; which however
soon gave place to that of hopeful encouragement,
as he joyfully recognized the fruitful effects of
the varied efforts put forth by many of its
members.

Perhaps of few it could be said with more
truth, he coveted no man's silver or gold or
apparel, that his hands ministered to his own and

his neighbour's necessities; * whilst his humble Christian walk, and large-hearted hospitality, tended in more ways than one to support the weak; and to point, amongst his more intimate friends, to the blessings which may be realized in a life unfettered by the undue care of earthly things.

MARY BRANTINGHAM,   41 26   4 mo. 1870
  Kinmuck, Aberdeenshire.   An Elder.

EDWARD BREWIN,   59 11   9 mo. 1870
  Anstey Grange, Leicester.   A Minister.

If the subject of the following short sketch were present now, his earnest request would probably be, that any notice of his life and death should be very simple and very brief; consequently those who knew and loved him best, feel that they are bound to conform as much as possible to what they know would have been his desire in this respect. At the same time, Edward Brewin's life was so strikingly pervaded by the spirit of his Divine master, and formed such a beautiful example of a Christian's daily walk with God, that they think it would scarcely be right to omit some allusion to him in the pages of the *Annual Monitor.* Until nineteen years of age, he remained at his parental home in Cirencester,

---

* See the 20th Chapter of the Acts.

when he removed to Worcester; and although he was ever a loving and dutiful son, yet it was not till the period of manhood that there appeared much evidence of religious life. He spent many years of usefulness in Worcester, exemplifying Christian assiduity, both in his religious and temporal engagements. He was acknowledged a Minister at about the age of thirty. During the latter part of his life he was a member of Leicester Meeting; where he was much beloved, and his ministerial gift very frequently exercised.

Edward Brewin was of a singularly guileless and simple nature; receiving with a grateful heart all temporal blessings, and submitting with child-like humility, when the hand of affliction was laid upon him. The theme upon which his mind delighted to dwell, was the love of God in Christ Jesus; and the peace and joy of the child of God were very often the subjects of his ministry. His faith was beautifully simple, but strong and clear; enabling him to carry out any work which he undertook, with unwavering confidence. His sympathies were freely given to Christians of every name, and he was far more quick to recognize points of union than of difference. In social life there was much to endear him to those with whom he came in contact. Whilst habitually sincere in word and manner, his unselfish nature prompted him never to forget the little courtesies of life ; which he rendered alike to old and young, rich and poor.

He was frequently occupied in ministerial service away from home, visiting the meetings of Friends in various parts of England, and holding meetings with others in towns or country villages. In the latter work he was often engaged when at home ; and he had intended to have been present at a meeting in a small village near his residence, on the afternoon of his death. We believe his labours of this kind were much valued, and truly blessed. One striking feature of Edward Brewin's daily life should not be overlooked. It was his uniform practice to spend a considerable time in private retirement, especially in the early part of the day ; and he loved to occupy in this way, the quiet hours of a summer's morning.

His death was so sudden that there is no lengthened illness to record ; in fact, neither he nor his friends were aware of his danger till the end came. In his case, it was indeed a transition from time to eternity with no consciousness of the dark valley which lies between :—consequently to those around him, it is the *life* rather than the death, which has left the deepest impression. In the home where his last days were spent, he has left a bright example and a hallowed memory. The poor, amongst whom he especially laboured, have lost a true friend ; and in that portion of the church of which he was a member, he is sincerely mourned.

MARY JANE O'BRIEN,   18 14   6 mo. 1870
    Liverpool.   Daughter of John G. and Hannah O'Brien.

EDWARD BROOK, *Wakefield.*   60   2 12 mo. 1869

HARRIET BROTHERS,   84   7 12 mo. 1869
    York, formerly Bristol.

HANNAH BURGESS,   73 25   9 mo. 1870
    Stoke Newington.   Widow of John Funston Burgess.

SAMUEL BURLINGHAM,   78 26   3 mo. 1870
    Malvern Link.

WILLIAM BURTON,   63 11 10 mo. 1869
    Crawshawbooth, Lancashire.

WILLIAM BUTLER, *Bristol.*   74 30   9 mo. 1870

ELIZABETH CANDLER,   82 10   1 mo. 1870
    Bawburgh, near Norwich.   Sister of the late John Candler.

      E. Candler was from an early age occupied in teaching, in which she was very skilful, and gained the esteem and love of many, whose friendship continued through life. She had a well-stored and versatile mind, and was an occasional contributor to the periodicals which circulate amongst Friends, and to other kindred publications. She ever manifested much interest in Christian doctrine, and evinced a concern that Scriptural truth should be clearly apprehended. She was a diligent reader of the Bible, and one who truly feared to offend God. It is believed a little incident in her early childhood had a lasting effect on her character. On one occasion, she yielded to the temptation of telling a falsehood. Her parents at once separated her for two days from the other children: and their serious and united efforts to convince her of the sinfulness of her conduct, left an impression on her mind that was never forgotten.

Her views were remarkably independent. She seldom spoke of her inmost feelings: but was highly conscientious, strict and devout in her religious duties; a growing Christian. Some one speaking of the duty of *vocal* prayer, she said, " I pray as I walk about." A religion of *mere* conscientiousness did not satisfy either her understanding or her heart. For exterior forms she had little esteem; and though adhering, from motives of convenience, to the distinctive costume of the Friend of forty years ago, she remarked that the *necessity* for outward peculiarity, "never found place in her mind."

Her last moments were sweetly peaceful; her mind being stayed, and her hopes firmly resting on her Saviour. Her characteristic animation was maintained to the very end, and her mental powers appeared to be in no way impaired, at the solemn moment in which she breathed her last.

She left a memorandum behind her, by which to assure her surviving friends of her unfaltering trust in God, in spite of many perplexities ; and that she had a peaceful prospect of acceptance with Him, for the sake of a crucified Saviour, in whom all her trust was placed.

MARIA CANDLER,   78 13   3 mo. 1870
   Chelmsford.   Died at York.   Widow of John
   Candler.

HELEN CAPPER,   28 20   5 mo. 1870
   New Brighton, Liverpool.   Wife of Samuel
   James Capper.

MARY CAPPER,   85 17   8 mo. 1870
   Shirley, Southampton.   Widow   of   Jasper
   Capper.

MARY CARROLL,   83 8   7 mo. 1870
   Cork.   Widow of Thomas Carroll.

JOSEPH CASH, *Coventry.*   85 3   1 mo. 1870

Joseph Cash, the son of John and Elizabeth Cash, both Ministers, was born at Coventry in the year 1784. There are no special memoranda of his inner life, but a few extracts from his letters may give some insight into it; his outward life abundantly testifying to his discipleship, by the uniform consistency of his character, and his daily walk with God.

He had an humble opinion of his own attainments, but felt constrained by the love of Christ to invite his fellow-man to come and believe in Jesus, particularly dwelling upon the *fulness* of the Gospel message; having himself in early life sought acceptance with God by the performance of moral works, and having found them insufficient to give peace of mind.

In the years 1830 and 31 he was one of the Yearly Meeting's Committee appointed to visit the Quarterly meetings, and he seems to have had peaceful satisfaction in the service; remarking, " I am often baptized into much poverty of spirit under a deep sense of my utter unworthiness. Still the refreshing influence of my Saviour's love is vouchsafed to me at seasons, to the comforting of my weary soul; and I am enabled through His grace and good Spirit to cast my all into His hands, and to say ' Thy will be done.' "

On recovering from a severe illness, he says :
" I know myself to be unworthy of the notice of
my friends and neighbours : yet I have reason to
believe, their prayers and intercessions, offered on
my behalf when I was much prostrated, were,
under the blessing of a merciful and gracious
God, the means of my being raised up from a bed
of sickness." His love for the Scriptures was
deep and reverent. On one occasion he writes :
" I feel it my required duty to give much time to
the reading of them : praying to my heavenly
Father for the guidance of the Holy Spirit, that
I might more fully understand these inestimable
records of the will of God ; for I find the more I
become acquainted with them, the more I love
them."

He thus alludes to his early training respecting the indwelling and guidance of the Spirit of
Truth : " Even from my very early youth this
was inculcated by the tender care of pious parents ;
and, through the continued blessing of my gracious
God and Saviour, was never more firmly believed
in, than at the present time. Perhaps few individuals have carried this conviction of the important agency of the Holy Spirit further than
I have, and yet I think not further than sacred
Scripture warrants. I have not confined its

operation and guidance to merely scriptural truths ; but have believed those individuals who love and serve God, are also favoured with its gracious help, in directing their movements in the outward avocations of the present life : and I consider this a very high and merciful privilege."

About the time of his middle life, our Society was much agitated by controversy : when his advanced views of Gospel truth were misunderstood by some of his friends. This deeply pained his sensitive mind; but he did not feel at liberty to withdraw from the Society, believing it would ultimately more fully recognize Evangelical truth. On one occasion he writes : " What joy is there to be compared with the joy of God's salvation ! what peace to be compared with that peace which the believer has in Jesus! What hope is like unto that hope which is afforded in the Gospel !"

Thus at the end of a long pilgrimage he was prepared, through the mercy of God in Christ Jesus, to enter that city, that " needeth not the light of the sun, neither of the moon, to shine in it : for the glory of God doth lighten it, and the Lamb is the light thereof."

Lydia Casson, *York.*   29   5   2 mo. 1870

WILLIAM HENRY CATCHPOOL, 1¼ 29 9 mo. 1869
Islington, London. Son of William and Sarah
Catchpool.

EDITH MARIA CATCHPOOL,   15 8 12 mo. 1869
Reading. Daughter of Richard Davison and
Sarah Catchpool.

JULIA CATLIN,   41 24 8 mo. 1870
Whitechapel. Daughter of Jane and the late
John Hallam Catlin.

ROBERT CHARNLEY,   71 6 5 mo. 1870
Preston in Lancashire.

SARAH CHRIMES,   64 14 9 mo. 1870
Fulshaw, Wilmslow. Wife of Joseph Chrimes.

MARY CLIBBORN, *Moate.*   72 18 3 mo. 1870

THOMAS CLIBBORN, *Moate.* 71 27 5 mo. 1870

DOROTHY COATES,   69 27 4 mo. 1870
Smelt House, Bishop Auckland.

GRACE COCKBURN-CAMPBELL, 65 31 7 mo. 1870
Waterhead, Windermere. Interred at Colthouse.
Wife of Sir Alexander T. Cockburn-Campbell,
Bart.

EDWARD COLCOCK, *Andover.* — 13 10 mo. 1869

ANNA COLEMAN,   77 8 7 mo. 1870
Wandsworth, London. Wife of Robert Coleman.

JANE COLLIER,   94 16 6 mo. 1870
Woodside, Plymouth.

ELIZABETH COOK,   71 25 12 mo. 1869
Rochester. Daughter of Mary Cook, of London.

HENRY CRAWFORD,   85 24 10 mo. 1869
    Gorton, near Manchester.

EDMUND CREETH,   40 4 2 mo. 1870
    Pendleton, Manchester.

MARTHA CROSLAND,   48 18 1 mo. 1870
    Worcester. A Minister. Wife of Joseph
    Crosland.

MARY ANN CROSSLAND,   78 13 11 mo. 1869
    Plaistow.

ISABELLA CULLIMORE,   71 14 10 mo. 1869
    Belfast.

CHISLEU CUMINE,   76 27 9 mo. 1869
    London. Wife of Francis Cumine.

FRANCIS CUMINE,   83 25 11 mo. 1869
    Pontefract, late of London.

WILLIAM HARTAS DALE,   1¾ 5 6 mo. 1870
    Danby, Guisbro'. Son of Richard and Sarah
    Mary Dale.

LUCY DARBY,   89 10 5 mo. 1870
    Ebbw Vale. Widow of Edmund Darby.

ANN DARTON,   82 27 11 mo. 1869
    Stoke Newington. Widow of Samuel Darton.

JAMES EDWARD DAWES,   43 25 9 mo. 1870
    Stoke Newington. Died at York.

SARAH DEANE,   69 26 11 mo. 1869
    Reigate. Wife of James Deane.

CHARLES DELL,   61 2 12 mo. 1869
    Bluntisham, near Earith.

SARAH JANE DICKINSON,   35 29 4 mo. 1870
Whitehaven.   Daughter of Isaac and Lucy
Dickinson.

JANE DICKINSON,   93 4 5 mo. 1870
Maryport.   Widow of John Dickinson.

ANN DICKINSON,   78 17 6 mo. 1870
Highflatts.   Widow of Richard Dickinson.

MARGARET DIXON.   66 9 5 mo. 1870
Darlington.

JOSEPH DOUBLEDAY,   20 9 1 mo. 1870
Sunderland.   Son of William and Maria
Doubleday, of Coggeshall.

During the short and unexpected illness
which terminated the earthly course of this young
disciple of Jesus, he was preserved in much
quietness and sweetness of spirit. He expressed
his feeling of unworthiness; but having given
his heart to Christ, he was enabled to rest in His
love, saying on one occasion, "I do love Him,"
and several times, "I am so happy," and when
near his end, "Underneath are the everlasting
arms."

HANNAH JANE DOUGLAS.   6½ 13 7 mo. 1870
Dublin.   Daughter of John Douglas.

MARY JANE DOYLE,   29 11 2 mo. 1870
Cork.   Daughter of Joshua Doyle.

HENRY DREWETT,   68 17 2 mo. 1870
Felsted, Essex.

ELLEN DYMOND, 42 22 10 mo. 1869
  Birmingham. Wife of George Dymond.
MARY EDDINGTON, 4 27 1 mo. 1870
  Worcester. Daughter of W. C. & H. Eddington.
ANNE EDMUNDS, 41 18 7 mo. 1870
  Peckham. Wife of William Edmunds.
JANE EDMUNDSON, 57 21 1 mo. 1870
  Kingstown, near Dublin.
MARGARET EDWARDS, 87 29 3 mo. 1870
  Lanthewy Court, Monmouthshire.
FRANK ELGAR, 10 15 9 mo. 1870
  Canterbury. Son of John and Elizabeth Elgar.
WILLIAM KEMP EVANS, 76 17 6 mo. 1870
  Wormley, near Hoddesdon, Hertfordshire.
ABIGAIL EVANS, 65 15 9 mo. 1870
  Westburn, Limerick. Widow of James P.
  Evans.
MARY ANN FARDON, 23 23 4 mo. 1870
  Stockton on Tees. Wife of Joseph Henry
  Fardon.
ELIZA FENNELL, 81 8 12 mo. 1869
  Cottage, near Cahir. Widow of George Fennell.
JOSEPH FIRTH, *Dewsbury.* 69 8 9 mo. 1870
ROBERT FLETCHER, *Dewsbury.* 66 28 10 mo. 1869
SARAH FLOUNDERS, 89 12 4 mo. 1870
  Great Ayton, Guisbro'
JOHN JAMES FOX, *Devizes.* 65 27 10 mo. 1869

D

JOSIAH FORSTER,   88 27 6 mo. 1870
  Tottenham.   An Elder. *

EMILY FOWLER,   26 30 12 mo. 1869
  Gloucester.   Wife of Edward Fowler.

WALTER GAWEN FRY,   31 19 5 mo. 1870
  Cotham, Bristol.   Third son of Francis and
  Matilda Fry.

ELIZABETH PEASE FRY,   40 27 9 mo. 1870
  Clifton, Bristol.   Wife of Lewis Fry.

AGNES GARDNER, *Leeds.*   1½ 21 4 mo. 1870
  Daughter of Richard Dawson and Elizabeth
  Jane Gardner.

JOSEPH GIBBINS,   84 24 3 mo. 1870
  Houndshill, near Stratford on Avon.

MARY GILKES, *Reading.*   84 25 1 mo. 1870

JOHN GILLETT,   68 17 12 mo. 1869
  Cheltenham, late of Brails.

EDWIN GILMORE,   21 2 12 mo. 1869
  Belfast.   Son of William Gilmore.

MARY ANN GODLEE,   73 21 8 mo. 1870
  Lewes.   An Elder.

RACHEL GOOSE,   73 19 8 mo. 1870
  Norwich.   Widow of Robert Goose.

HANNAH GOULDING,   55 2 1 mo. 1870
  Hyde Park, Cork.   Wife of H. M. Goulding.

ELIZABETH GRAY,   86 5 12 mo. 1869
  Chelsea.   Widow of John Gray.

               * See the end of this Obituary.

THOMAS GRAY,   52 24   5 mo. 1870
  Kentish Town, London.

RACHEL REED GRAY,   34   1   8 mo. 1870
  Stoke Newington.   Widow of George Gray.

ANNA MARY GREEN,   24   6   2 mo. 1870
  Belfast.   Daughter of Forster and Mary Green.

ELIZA HEWETT GREGORY,   58 22   9 mo. 1869
  Basingstoke.   *(Name reported last year.)*

The life of this beloved friend was marked by that unceasing flow of little kindnesses and gentle deeds, which can only proceed from a heart filled with affection and sympathy. Pleasing manners and a natural cheerfulness of disposition made her a very general favourite; and many, both within her own immediate circle of friends, and beyond it, have borne testimony to her piety, her loving spirit, and her fitness for the educational duties to which the last twenty years of her life were devoted.

Endowed with a large measure of that beautiful and simple wisdom which makes neither noise nor appearance, she was eminently qualified to be " a teacher of babes." In this occupation she found a large field of usefulness, and laboured therein with a zealous and affectionate interest: it was her delight to take her young charge by the hand, in the bright spring-tide of their existence,

and lead them to the feet of Jesus, so that the
injunction " Feed my lambs " might, so far as
lay in her power, be faithfully obeyed.   Some
little verses, pen-printed by her on a card, and
given to each of her pupils, expresses in a few
simple words the lessons she loved to teach
them :—

Wise men of old to Bethlehem came
   To seek the Son of God :
A manger was His resting-place,
   A stable His abode :
The treasures of the East they bring
To offer to their Heavenly King.

Gold from the cavern's dark retreat,
   Myrrh from the waving grove,
And frankincense, an offering meet
   As tributes of their love ;
Now what can little children bring
To offer to their Heavenly King ?

He loves a little tender heart
   Filled with affections kind,
Which seeks Him as the better part,
   Seeks, with desire to find ;
This heart may little children bring
An offering to their Heavenly King.

Throughout the long illness which preceded her death, she was preserved in a state of calm and peaceful resignation : the sense of her own unworthiness seemed swallowed up in an assurance of the all-sufficiency of Infinite Love ; and thus, enabled with a child-like trust to appropriate the promises, she was favoured with a foretaste of that Rest which remaineth for the people of God.

During the last few days of her life, when weakness and suffering increased, she sometimes expressed a desire to be released, but was very patient, and gratefully acknowledged every little service or alleviation rendered. As the close drew near, she was too weak to express much ; but the sudden radiance on the face, and the words " very near heaven," twice repeated, spoke comfort to the mourners who stood by her dying bed and received her last sigh !

Farewell, beloved sister and friend ! when the solemn hour arrives to us which must arrive to all, may it be our privilege, as it was thine, to feel that we are " *Very near Heaven !*"

JAMES GREGORY,   77 19 10 mo. 1869
    Evesham.

SARAH GREGORY,   78 16 12 mo. 1869
    Street, in Somersetshire.   An Elder.

MARY GREGORY,   52 15   5 mo. 1870
   Yatton, near Bristol.   Daughter of Maurice
and Phœbe Gregory.

THOMAS GRIMES,   70 5   4 mo. 1869
   Cranfield, near Newport Pagnell.

ANNE GRIMES, *Bix Oxon.*   34 30   6 mo. 1870

ERNEST GRIMSHAW, *London.* 21 15   9 mo. 1870
   Son of Frederick and Harriet Grimshaw.

JOHN GRUBB,   53 13   3 mo. 1870
   Deer Park, near Carrick-on-Suir.

ELIZABETH GULSON,   95 18   5 mo. 1870
   Oadley Hill, Leicester.   Widow of John Gulson.

THOMAS HAGEN, *Carlisle.*   82 2   3 mo. 1870
   An Elder.

ELIZA HAIGH, *Holmfirth.*   50 19   6 mo. 1870
   Wife of Joshua Haigh.

SAMUEL HALL, *Folkstone.*   82 21   7 mo. 1870

JOHN F. HALLIDAY,   1¼ 9   2 mo. 1870
   Drumgask, Lurgan.   Son of James Halliday.

ABRAHAM HANSON,   50 4   4 mo. 1870
   Huddersfield.

GEORGE HARRIS, *Cork.*   66 16   8 mo. 1869

HENRIETTA HARRIS,   7 3   2 mo. 1870
   Bessbrook, near Newry.   Daughter of John
Frederick and Elizabeth Harris.

CHARLOTTE HARRIS,   77 10   4 mo. 1870
   Walthamstow.   Widow of Joseph Owen Harris.

ELIZABETH HARRISSON, 58 3 9 mo. 1870
Willow Cottage, Earl's Colne. Wife of Francis
Harrisson.

RACHEL HARTAS, 75 16 1 mo. 1870
Danby, Guisbro'. Widow of William Hartas.

ROBERT HARTLEY, *Kendal.* 81 3 1 mo. 1870

SARAH HAUGHTON, 75 5 12 mo. 1869
Greenbank, Carlow. Widow of Thomas
Haughton.

MARY HAYCOCK, *Worcester.* 86 6 1 mo. 1870

JOHN GEORGE HAYMAN, 67 9 8 mo. 1870
Dorking.

JOHN HEWARD, *Hull.* 83 18 12 mo. 1869

JANE HEWITSON, 95 5 5 mo. 1870
Headingley, Leeds. Widow of John Hewitson.

CONSTANCE ANNIE HICKS, 10 mos. 4 5 mo. 1870

ADA HARRIET HICKS, 7 7 7 mo. 1870
Springfield, Chelmsford. Children of Henry
(Jr.) and Sarah Hicks.

SARAH HILL, 83 11 10 mo. 1869
Plaistow.

FRANCIS HOBSON, 68 16 5 mo. 1870
Drumanoey, County Tyrone. An Elder.

THOMAS HODGSON, 69 23 10 mo. 1869
York, formerly of Bentham.

SARAH HODGSON, 63 19 8 mo. 1870
Wilderspool, near Warrington.

ELIZABETH HOLMES,   70   3   2 mo. 1870
 Newcastle-on-Tyne. Widow of William Holmes.
JOHN HOLDSWORTH,   60   5   1 mo. 1870
 Eccles, Manchester. Died at Ramleh, in Egypt,
and interred at Mentone, by Nice.
WILLIAM HOOD, *Selby.*   54   5   7 mo. 1870
MARY ANN HORNE,   79 13   9 mo. 1870
 Clapham.   Widow of James Horne.
JOHN HORNBY,   83   2   8 mo. 1870
 Thornton Marsh, near Blackpool.
CLARA JANE HORSNAILL,   20 24   2 mo. 1870
 Rochester. Daughter of Alfred and Jane Bevans
Horsnaill.
ELIZABETH HOWARD,   90 15 12 mo. 1869
 Bruce Grove, Tottenham. Widow of Thomas
Howard.
ANNE HUGHES,   76 20 10 mo. 1869
 Kingstown, Dublin.   Daughter of Joseph
Hughes, late of Clonmel.
WILLIAM HENRY HURTLEY,   10 28 12 mo. 1869
 Malton.   Son of Dickinson and Mary Hurtley.
GERALD HUTCHINSON,   2¾ 23   9 mo. 1870
 Selby.   Son   of   Charles   and   Elizabeth
Hutchinson.
JAMES INGHAM,   78 25   7 mo. 1870
 Batley, Dewsbury.
MARY IMPEY, *Berkhamstead.* 71 29 12 mo. 1869

HANNAH IMPEY, 75 3 9 mo. 1870
Sudbury. A Minister. Widow of William
Impey, of Earl's Colne.

EMMA LOUISA JACKSON, 5 9 5 mo. 1870
Ashton-on-Mersey. Daughter of William and
Agatha Suddens Jackson.

SUSAN MATILDA JACKSON, 24 10 5 mo. 1870
Banvale, Moyallon. Youngest daughter of the
late John Pim Jackson.

MARIA JACOB, 86 8 3 mo. 1870
Waterford. An Elder. Widow of Joseph
Jacob.

This dear friend acceptably occupied the
important station of Elder in the church during
many of the latter years of her life, and in the
performance of the duties connected therewith
she endeavoured to be faithful.

Her last illness appeared to be a gradual
decline of bodily strength, previous to which she
was remarkable for her interest in passing events,
in the Temperance cause and other philanthropic
movements of the day; but especially in the
concerns of our Religious Society, the welfare
of which was dear to her heart. She was
endued with an excellent understanding, well
cultivated, and was deservedly beloved and
respected.

ELIZA JELLICO,	77	15	1 mo. 1870
Mountmellick.			
THOMAS JESPER,	69	30	12 mo. 1869
Warwick.			
GROVER KEMP,	77	21	12 mo. 1869

Brighton.   A Minister.

We have much satisfaction in preserving in our pages a memorial of this beloved friend, who from the first publication of the *Annual Monitor* highly valued its purpose and object, and looked with renewed interest for each succeeding volume.

Grover Kemp was the eldest son of John and Benjamina Kemp, and was born at Bermondsey in the outskirts of London, on the 10th of Ninth month, 1792. In early life, he was timid and thoughtful, and when scarcely seven years old, lost his mother : but at that early age had received from her affectionate lips lessons of heavenly wisdom from the pages of Holy Scripture, which he often gratefully alluded to, when himself the father of a family.

After his mother's death, the father going abroad, he was with his sister Benjamina received into the family of his maternal grandfather, Joseph Rickman of Staines. Here the two orphans experienced the watchful care of their aunt Mary Rickman, who sought to imbue their

young minds with the fear of the Lord and the
love of Jesus.*

While very young, Grover Kemp was sent to
a large school at Earl's Colne in Essex, conducted by the late John Kirkham, where his
sensitive nature had much to contend with, from
being thrown among companions considerably
older and more robust than himself. His
education was afterwards carried on at Hitchin
and Epping. At the age of fourteen, he was
apprenticed to John Glaisyer, chemist and drug-
gist at Brighton, with whom he subsequently
became a partner. He continued his connexion
with the same business until his retirement, about
six years before his decease : combining through
life the character of an upright and active
tradesman, with that of a devoted and ready
Christian.

Being fond of study, and feeling the dis-
advantage of having left school so young, he
endeavoured, during his apprenticeship, by early
rising, to find time for acquiring a knowledge of
chemistry, so necessary in his business ; also

* See an account of Benjamina Kemp, afterwards Penney,
in the *Annual Monitor* for 1868, and of Mary Rickman, afterwards Binns, in that for 1852. John Kemp in later life was
located near his son, who cared for and watched over him
till his decease in 1827.

to improve himself in French, and gain some acquaintance with the Greek language. He practised essay-writing when quite young; and some of these juvenile productions evinced much serious thoughtfulness.

While he has not left much record of his early religious struggles, there are a few memoranda of this nature. In his sixteenth year, on the death of his grandmother, he was led to reflect on the end of life, and the necessity of being always ready for it. "While in serious retirement on this awful event," he writes, "I have earnestly desired I may be prepared to meet the solemn change, since we know not in what day or hour our Lord may come : but his command was—(and may I be continually concerned to keep it,)—' Watch and pray, lest ye enter into temptation.' But alas! I fear I am too negligent in this most important of duties."

Under date of Eighth month, 28th, 1809, when nearly seventeen, he wrote,—" O how ardently desirous have I this day been, to be able sincerely and unequivocally to say with the Psalmist, "As the hart panteth after the waterbrooks, so panteth my soul after Thee, O God!— but alas! ' the spirit indeed is willing, but the flesh is weak.' "

He was married in 1816 to Susannah, eldest daughter of Robert and Elizabeth Horne of Arundel, and their union proved a happy one for more than fifty years. As a parent he manifested a most loving and tender affection. He was ever anxious to promote the highest interests of his children, and to instruct them in those views of Christian truth which he had himself embraced, and to which he was so closely attached. On returning from his long journeys in the service of the Gospel, he would enliven the family circle by graphic details, combining interesting information and amusing incidents of travel with instruction on subjects of higher moment. At the time when he was closely engaged in business behind a retail counter, it was his custom to withdraw for a short time in the course of the day for religious retirement, which doubtless contributed to his spiritual help and strength. And his punctual attendance through life of week-day meetings and those for discipline, tended to the same end.

It is believed his voice was first heard in the ministry in his nineteenth year in a Preparative Meeting, and from that time occasionally in the family circle. In his twenty-seventh year he spoke as a minister in a meeting for worship; and

E

was recorded as such by Lewes and Chichester Monthly Meeting in 1823.

He entered upon this solemn engagement with a deep conviction of its responsibility, and the necessity of being himself baptized of the Holy Spirit, before he could "speak baptizingly to others." His Gospel labours were varied and extensive, and continued over a term of nearly fifty years: during the whole of which time he was a member of Brighton meeting.

In the changing conditions of society, there are in the County of Sussex, as in other parts of England, various old meeting-houses that have been closed, in consequence of Friends no longer residing near; and it was a prominent engagement with our dear Friend to hold meetings in these deserted buildings with the inhabitants of the neighbourhood. Such a service was one of the first for which he sought the sanction of his Monthly meeting; and, besides other instances, on about twenty different occasions in the course of thirty-five years, did he go forth specially on this errand, with the approval of his friends. "In my feeble movements in Gospel service," he says in one of his letters, "I have felt a lively interest in our closed meeting-houses, with a desire that they may be at times rightly opened for worship

in our simple, but as I believe, proper way :"—
and he was much gratified towards the end of his
life, on hearing that some of them were about to
be regularly so opened.

Grover Kemp often held meetings in the
villages round Brighton in barns and store-
houses; and during the formation of the London
and Brighton, as well as of the Lewes and
Hastings railways, he had several meetings with
the men employed on the lines. He visited at
various times all the meetings of Friends in
England, except those of two Quarterly meetings
in the West, and very frequently, during these
visits, embraced opportunities for religious labour
among the poorer classes of the population : as for
instance at one time in the Potteries, at another
among the pitmen in some colliery districts;
others with the artizans of Birmingham, and
some in the densely populated districts of Rat-
cliffe and Wapping.

It is believed that his plain and simple
manner of setting religious truth before the
people was often blessed to them; and the Gospel
preached was felt to be the power of God unto
salvation. Often did he dwell on the encouragement offered to the " honest-hearted," and to
those who were endeavouring, amid many trials,

to live a pious and Christian life : handing the word of loving sympathy to the humble followers of a crucified, risen, and glorified Saviour.

In 1832, he visited the Friends in the south of France; and five years later spent many weeks, accompanied by his kind friend and fellow-townsman Isaac Bass, in a visit to the meetings of Friends in Ireland. In 1839, he visited the families of Friends in Dublin; and a similar mission took him in 1843 to Manchester, Liverpool, and Birmingham. These engagements were undertaken in dependence on heavenly aid, and the gracious Master, who called him to the work, gave ability "rightly to divide the word;" and in many a home the message of encouragement, or even warning, found a willing reception.

His beloved friend John Marsh of Dorking accompanied him to the Isle of Man in 1855, and the year following he visited the Scilly Islands. In a visit to the Channel Islands he held many public meetings, not omitting the smaller islands, as well as Jersey and Guernsey.

The winter of 1857 and 58 was spent in some of the West Indian Islands, in company with his youngest son, and his valued friend William Holmes of Alton. The object particularly in view was to hold meetings with the free black population; and in this he was very cordially and efficiently assisted by the missionaries residing in the islands, who freely offered him the use of their chapels. The large gatherings, sometimes comprising seven or eight hundred and upwards of negroes, were often seasons of Divine favour. With many of the missionaries Grover Kemp felt united in much Christian fellowship. On the 24th of Second month, 1858, he writes in the island of Trinidad: " To-morrow we shall I believe be launched on the mighty deep on our homeward voyage. May the Lord Almighty mercifully protect and preserve us. I feel my mind graciously covered with that calming peace which is not at our command, breathing gratitude and praise to Him, who has so marvellously and mercifully brought us through this arduous engagement :—to whom belongs all the glory and all the praise." A few days later, on board the steamer, he wrote, " It is a great favour, in passing these islands which have been the scene of our Gospel labours, to feel so sweetly and peacefully clear of them,—not the weight of a feather resting on the mind respecting them."

The last certificate granted our dear friend was in 1862, for religious service in the Eastern Counties, embracing family visits to Friends in

Ipswich. In the early part of 1863, he formed one of the Yearly Meeting's Committee to visit the Quarterly Meetings ; and while uniting with other Friends in Bedfordshire and Hertfordshire, his health gave way, and on his return home a serious illness of several months ensued.

The time for extended labour was now over. His health was however again restored ; and being relieved from the cares of business, and from the wide field of religious service over which he had travelled, he still employed himself in attending to many objects in his own locality, which had claimed a share of his attention for many years. He was one of the first and most earnest supporters of a Savings' Bank in Brighton at its establishment in 1817, and continued his periodical attendance there while ability lasted. He was remarkably punctual and reliable in all he undertook, and often rendered material assistance in the character of a Trustee. He was, with other well-wishers to his country, a friend and supporter of the Temperance cause, and some years ago wrote an earnest appeal, called "*A Tract for the Season*," in reference to the revelling and license that many indulge in, at the time called Christmas. Many copies were distributed by the Town Missionary, and it can still be had from the Brighton Friends' Tract Association.*

His ministry continued to animate and comfort his friends; and, as they testify, he laboured amongst them, " often with a mental power and doctrinal clearness fully equal to the days of his meridian strength." Yet his habitual humility is exhibited in a few lines addressed, on the return of his birth-day in 1864, to his beloved friend Daniel Pryor Hack, with whom he had long been intimately connected in social and religious fellowship. " 12th of Ninth month. On Seventh Day last I completed my 72nd year. * * I desire to commemorate the many blessings and favours of which I have been the unworthy receiver. 'Surely goodness and mercy have followed me all the days of my life:' but oh! how short of the mark I have been in many ways through unwatchfulness! I have nothing to trust to, or depend upon, but the mercy of God in Christ Jesus, for the forgiveness of my sins of omission and commission, and acceptance in Him the Beloved."

In the year 1869, he spent some weeks in Birmingham, watching with others of his family the gradual decline of his youngest daughter,

* Price 1s. 6d. per 100, or 13s. per 1000, post free.

Susanna H. Barrow: but while mourning the loss of this beloved one, he could rejoice in the sweet assurance, granted to the survivors, of her admittance within the "pearl gates."

Shortly after, while attending his own Quarterly Meeting, he was again laid up with illness, at the residence of his kind friends Sarah Shepherd and Elizabeth Bell, at Alton in Hampshire. It was about three weeks before he sufficiently recovered to undertake the return journey to Brighton: and after this he was very much confined to the house; though able to join his friends on three occasions at their meeting for worship. The following account has been preserved of his last public address in the ministry. "He rose with the words addressed by the Apostle Paul to the Elders of Ephesus, when he had told them that they should see his face no more,—'And now, brethren, I commend you to God, and to the word of His grace, which is able to build you up, and to give you an inheritance among all them that are sanctified.' A lively testimony to the Truth followed: and although feeble in body, yet after having sat down he rose again; and as if to remind his hearers once more of a truth which it had often been his concern to enforce, he said, 'This then is the message, which we have heard of Him and declare unto you, that God is light, and in Him is no darkness at all. If we say that we have fellowship with Him, and walk in darkness, we lie, and do not the truth :—but if we walk in the light, as He is in the light, we have fellowship one with another, and the blood of Jesus Christ his Son cleanseth us from all sin.' " (1 John i. 5-7.)

Towards the end of the Eleventh month, his illness increased, and his sufferings were often great: but they were borne with much Christian patience, and repeated evidence was given of his firm faith in the Redeemer, and of the joyful prospect that was before him, of being with his Lord for ever.

On the 3rd of Twelfth month, he offered a very sweet prayer, asking that he might be upheld when passing through the valley of the shadow of death, and for the support of his dear wife, if he should be taken from her. He afterwards spoke of his unworthiness, that he had been an unprofitable servant, but that his trust was in the dear Saviour. He expressed his need of patience ; and, on being reminded of his beloved daughter's words, " if I am kept in patience, it is not of myself," he said emphatically, " that is very true."

On the 20th, the last evening which he spent
on earth, he said, " I am peaceful and happy,
trusting in the Lord and the dear Saviour."
When arranging for the night, he engaged in
prayer, using these expressions : " Forgive me all
my sins for Thy dear Son's sake. I am utterly
unworthy : oh, in Thine own good time, take me
to Thyself. Thy time is the best time." In less
than twelve hours his wish was fulfilled. The
prayer was answered. Nearly the last words he
uttered were, " Lord, now lettest Thou Thy
servant depart in peace, for mine eyes have seen
Thy salvation :" and it is reverently believed the
redeemed Spirit was blessed with an entrance
into that glorious City, which " hath no need of
the sun, neither of the moon, to shine in it : for
the glory of God doth lighten it, and the Lamb is
the light thereof."

RICHARD HENRY KEYMER, 37 13 2 mo. 1870
   York, formerly Cirencester.

EDWARD KING, *York.* 46 23 11 mo. 1869

JOHN KING, 84 24 6 mo. 1870
   Moss Side, Manchester.

ELIZABETH KNIGHT, 61 19 10 mo. 1869
   Kettering.

HANNAH MARY KNIGHT, 5½ 3 1 mo. 1870
   Northfleet, Rochester. Daughter of John
Messer and Hannah Knight.

FREDERICK JOSEPH KNIGHT, 19 12   1 mo. 1870
  Margate.   Son of Alfred and Susan Lucy
  Knight.

ANNE LAMB,   69 25   1 mo. 1870
  Bloomfield, Dublin.

JOSHUA LAMB,   75 11   7 mo. 1870
  Sibford, Ferris.   A Minister.

ELLEN LAMB,   30 20   7 mo. 1870
  Birmingham.   Daughter of Joseph and Eleanor
  Lamb.

RICHARD LAMLEY,   88 4 11 mo. 1869
  Tredington, near Shipston-on-Stour.

ELIZABETH LEAFE,   85 8   1 mo. 1870
  Malton, Yorkshire.

WALTER LEAN,   2 22   4 mo. 1870
  Peckham Rye.   Son of Walter and Ellen
  Lean.

TOM TURNER LEATHER,   16 31 10 mo. 1869
  Burnley.   Son of Samuel Petty and Hannah
  Leather.

DONALD LENNOX,   23 16   3 mo. 1870
  Ullermire, near Kirklinton, Cumberland.

JOSEPH JACKSON LISTER, F.R.S.,
  Upton House, Plaistow.   83 24 10 mo. 1869

SARAH LITTLEBOY,   75 25   3 mo. 1870
  Berkhamstead.   A Minister.   Widow of
  William Littleboy.

In recording the decease of this dear friend, we think it right to bear our testimony to the work of Grace, by which she became a living witness to the Truth as it is in Jesus.

She was the daughter of John and Mary Eeles of Amersham, but was very early in life deprived of a mother's care. This great loss was in measure mitigated by the kindness of her maternal aunts, by whom she was trained in a circumspect and useful walk in life. She was married in 1817 to William Littleboy of Berkhamstead, by the death of whom in 1837 she was left a widow with six children. Though greatly feeling this heavy bereavement, it was borne with much Christian resignation, and she could acknowledge that from the first she had been enabled to say, "Thy will be done." Throughout her married life her mind was very preciously visited by the Holy Spirit, and she was early led to see, that her only hope rested on the free mercy of God in Christ Jesus.

From the copious memoranda left by our dear friend, we may gather the earnest solicitude she felt for the best welfare of her children ; and many were the prayers she uttered on their behalf. For many years, it had been her practice to set apart a portion of the day for private retirement; and we doubt not that strength was thus afforded for the important duties devolving upon her. She was well read in Holy Scripture, and was often engaged in recording her impressions of various texts which came under her consideration. She had a decided poetical talent, and in the many pieces of great interest which she penned, the great and glorious theme of a Saviour's love was almost invariably introduced. Her views on doctrinal subjects were very clear, and she was made helpful to many with whom she had religious intercourse.

Under date Twelfth month 22nd, 1839, she writes : " Amid the many anxious cares which often press heavily on my spirit, how precious is it in any degree to ' cast my burden on the Lord,' to pour out before Him my secret supplications and tears ! This I think I was in some measure enabled to do, in both our Meetings to-day. I felt an importunate solicitude for the salvation of my own soul, and the souls of my beloved children; with a deep sense of our utter helplessness, and dependence on the mercy of God in Christ Jesus." It was about this time, after much conflict of mind, and with a sense of exceeding weakness, that she yielded to a conviction that it was her duty to endeavour to pray

F

with her beloved family. From this time forward she very frequently availed herself of this blessed privilege ; and her children can bear testimony to the earnestness with which she poured out her heart in prayer and praise, committing them again and again to the free mercy of God in the Redeemer.

But it was not for her family alone that she was brought under religious exercise : she earnestly sought the temporal and spiritual wellbeing of those by whom she was surrounded, and was diligent in visiting and ministering to the necessities of the poor. For some years before her decease, our dear friend conducted a Mother's Meeting ; and great was her solicitude on behalf of those with whom she was thus brought into contact. Notwithstanding her advanced age, and the declining state of her health, she never relaxed in this effort for the good of her fellow creatures ; and the saddened countenances of the poor women who stood around the open grave, bore striking testimony to the hold she had obtained on their affections.

After the loss sustained by the little Meeting at Berkhamstead in the removal by death of her brother-in-law Thomas Squire in 1851, our dear friend felt it required of her to speak of the love and mercy of God in the redemption of fallen man, in our meetings for worship. This she continued throughout the remainder of her life, greatly to the comfort and edification of her friends. During the last few years these communications were especially clear and impressive, and her friends can testify to the evident ripening and growth in grace, with which she was favoured.

During the latter portion of her life our dear friend suffered from an affection of the heart, which was attended at times with alarming attacks on her breathing. She fully comprehended the serious character of her symptoms, and it was evident to all around her that she received it as a warning to prepare for the final summons. Within a few weeks of her decease she wrote as follows : " My precious children continue to pray for me that I may be supported to the end, which seems at times as if it could not be very distant; and oh that what I have so often spoken of to others may be realized in my own experience,—*that* victory over the last enemy, which our Divine Redeemer has purchased for the true believer." She earnestly counselled her children to the private and prayerful perusal of the Scriptures ; and bade them seek the help of the Holy Spirit, rightly to understand that which the same Holy Spirit put forth. She had interviews about this time with her servants, and with the Bible woman, whose work she had for years superintended;—administering to all words of counsel and encouragement, which will be long remembered by them.

A few days before the close she repeated the lines—

"I lay my sins on Jesus,
The spotless Lamb of God !
He bears them all, and frees us
From the accursed load."

Adding, "I am thankful I have laid mine on Him in days gone by; if I had not, I feel that nothing could be done now. 'He that is unjust, let him be unjust still.' I have cast myself so many times at my Saviour's feet, that I do believe, I *trust*, I do not wish to boast, that I am accepted by Him."

On the morning of the 25th of Third month about ten o'clock, she was permitted to pass away without a struggle, and was interred in Friends' Burial Ground at Berkhamstead, on the 1st of Fourth month.

We may properly conclude this notice of our

dear friend, by quoting the following lines from her pen, written expressly in reference to the little grave-yard in which her remains now rest.

"A few short years, not one can tell how soon!
And other graves shall open,—other groups
Of mourners gather round,—while thoughts, deep
  thoughts,
From memory's gushing fountain shall supply
Some hallowed drops to water the green sod.
So must, so let it be,—we say, Amen:
If Jesus be our refuge, all is well;
Our wearied bodies shall lie down in peace,
Our souls to Heaven ascend, and live with Him."

MARY LOBLEY,   68 27 1 mo. 1870
  Leeds. Wife of John Lobley.

SAMUEL LUCAS, *Hitchin.*   64 29 3 mo. 1870

MARY ANN LUSCOMBE,   66 26 2 mo. 1870
  Birkenhead. Wife of Henry Luscombe.

She was the eldest daughter of Peter and Deborah Kenway, of Bridport; and in a family of fourteen, she was in a remarkable degree beloved through life by every one of her nine brothers and four sisters. This may be largely attributed to her natural warmth of affection, and the influence of favourable circumstances; of her it may be emphatically said, "In her tongue was the law of kindness." Proverbs xxxi. 26. She was blessed with a happy home; and however any of that large family may have been scattered from the fold, in which they were fondly nurtured and carefully educated, as members of our Religious Society, there is not one of them who may read these lines, but will joyfully testify to the beauty of that picture of the home of their childhood. Mary Ann was ever ready to dilate with all the exuberance of her bright spirit, on the reminiscences of that period of gladness and of hopefulness. She constantly bore witness to the blessings of a guarded education; often calling to mind the wholesome restraints of parental watchfulness,—of school discipline,—and of advice administered by Friends: saying impressively; "My steps had almost gone, my feet had well nigh slipped."

It was her happy experience to be brought under the power of the Gospel,—under the teaching of Christ by his secret touches in the soul,—whilst she yet rejoiced in the dew of her youth; when she was described by her fond sister, next younger, as a vine whose luxuriant branches ran over the wall. Divine grace gave a new aspect to her character,—new aspirations,—new concern both for herself and others,—as well as new trials and exercises. To the natural,

unregenerate mind, the Son and sent of God has
no beauty that it should desire Him : and the
new birth is not accomplished without conflict.
The subject of this memoir received the truth in
the love of it, was blessed in faith and obedience,
and was made a blessing to others. Once, in the
prime and vigour of her day, she was addressed
by a Minister in the language of Divine promise,
"I will surely bless thee, and make thee a
blessing." This was abundantly fulfilled in her.

Not that she was exempt from trial and
suffering. She saw many changes, and perhaps
the most impressive and instructive page in her
history is that of her latter years, when visited
with sore affliction. During the last eleven years
of her life, she was unable, from the peculiar
local effects of a paralytic stroke, to express
anything in *articulate* language, or make known
her thoughts and wishes *either by speech or
writing*. She was however able to go about, and
enjoyed company ;—she retained her hearing and
perceptive faculties, and was able to travel and
visit her friends, using signs and motions, or
indistinct sounds, but deprived of the power of
utterance, or of inditing sentences.

Happy was it for her, and for those nearest
and dearest to her, that the patience and faith of

true discipleship then shone forth conspicuously. Then especially she bore the fruits of the Gospel of Christ, which she had received in early life. Then she remarkably evinced, that she had been Divinely taught, and was Divinely supported. Her mind was still bent upon what had been her encouraging example, as well as her precept on all occasions:—" To adorn the doctrine of God our Saviour in all things." She was thus enabled to bless the Lord in all her tribulation,—to hold forth the practical faith and patience of Jesus Christ,—to rejoice in the Lord,—and to count all things but loss, that she might win Christ, and be accepted by Him. Her end was peace.

MARY LYON,   52 5 5 mo. 1870
    Pemberton, near Wigan.

JANE MAFHAM,   73 18 5 mo. 1870
    Darlington. Widow of John Mafham.

EDWIN MARRIAGE,   25 6 8 mo. 1869
    Holloway, London. Son of Joseph and Eliza Marriage.

ROBERT MARSH, *Luton.*   58 4 12 mo. 1869

JOSEPH MARSH,   80 3 3 mo. 1870
    Bedford Park, Croydon.

SAMUEL MARSHALL,   78 3 11 mo. 1869
    Kendal. An Elder.

In tracing the life of this aged Christian, we have to speak of one who was a sound instructor of youth, a friend of science, a useful citizen, an active member of the Society of Friends, and a firm upholder of those views of Christian doctrine which distinguish them from other denominations. Many of our readers will, we doubt not, recal these prominent features of his character, and remember also the kindly word of salutary advice given in season, as of one who, " being dead, yet speaketh."

He was the son of Joseph and Jane Marshall, and was born in Leeds on the 27th of Fourth month 1790. He was educated at the Friends' school in that town, conducted by the late Joseph Tatham; among whose pupils were numbered not a few useful and distinguished members of our Society. Here Samuel Marshall first engaged in tuition, as an apprenticed assistant. In 1813, he took an usher's place in Joseph Crosfield's school at Hartshill in Warwickshire; and in 1815, at the age of 25, re-opened the Friends' school at Kendal, and entered on his life-work of 40 years in the education of 800 individuals; many of whom were accustomed to acknowledge, that they owed much of their success in life, as tradesmen and professional men, to the sound education, regular habits, and high principles inculcated by him.

This important undertaking was commenced in the fear of the Lord, and in dependence on the Divine blessing; as is manifested by the following prayer, found among his private papers after his death. "Unto Thee, and Thee only, O Lord, do I look for success in this new undertaking. If Thou, O Lord, see meet that it should not be successful, grant, I beseech Thee, strength to withstand the insinuations of the Evil one, that whatsoever I undertake, it may be to Thy praise. Amen. 30th of Sixth mo. 1815."—The success, thus reverently and submissively sought, was granted, and in the following year he began to receive boarders.

It was a time when the subject of popular education was claiming much attention, from the improved systems of Fellenberg and Pestalozzi. The culture of the understanding was being substituted for, or superadded to, the learning of lessons by rote; and the rudiments of natural philosophy were introduced, as an advance on the limited routine of the grammar schools and commercial academies. The attention of the Society of Friends was aroused to the importance of Scriptural study; and a course of such instruction was being commenced at Ackworth School, by the efforts of Joseph John Gurney.

Samuel Marshall had, during his two years at Hartshill, conducted a Bible Class for the benefit of his poorer neighbours:* and from the opening of his own boarding school at Kendal, he gave regular Scriptural instruction to his pupils. The Bible was read daily, though this was not then, as now, so extensively done in families: part of one afternoon in the week was devoted to explaining its truths and lessons; and on the first day of the week, he was similarly engaged, both with his own children and his pupils, being careful to show the Scriptural foundation of the religious views of Friends.

In 1819 he married Hannah Tipping of Whitehaven, of whom there is a brief testimony, drawn up by him, in the *Annual Monitor* of 1869. Their union extended over nearly fifty years. She was a loving companion and true helpmeet, uniting with him in his various benevolent endeavours to promote the welfare of others.

As their children grew up and their minds expanded, great was their father's solicitude on

---

* While residing here, he often, though a young man, sat down to worship in the old Meeting-house *alone*; but used in after life to recur to some of these solitary sittings, as times of peculiar blessing, and communion with God.

their behalf. Under date of 14th of Tenth month, 1835, he writes to one of them, " O the importance of being always on the watch ! for we know not when the messenger of death may be sent to us,—nor how soon.   Let us both, my dear child, often, very often, seek for ability to watch and pray, that through the mercy of God in Christ Jesus our Lord, we may be permitted to enter the Kingdom of Heaven, and live conformably to the Divine precepts and commands of our blessed Saviour.   What is it that we are to be ? *For ever with Him.* If so, we must obey His commands; —and the reward is, *for ever.* O the awful import of these words, '*for ever and ever !*'   Nothing, my dear child, would rejoice the hearts of thy dear mother and me so much, as to know that our dear children are endeavouring to prepare for a future state, by living in a watchful and prayerful frame of mind."

When about to place one of his sons in a business situation, he says : " I desire in this, as in all my movements, to be favoured with Divine direction to know how to act aright. I am most thoroughly convinced, that if we do but seek it, with a single eye to His glory, the Lord will guide us in all our ways, and help us to move consistently with His will ; *even in our outward concerns,* as well as in spiritual affairs. O how often do I wish that my children may now, in the morning of their days, seek to Him for direction in all their ways! and He will most assuredly guide their steps. What blessings then would He pour upon you, both temporal and spiritual!"

Thirty years later, in 1868, the same sentiment is expressed, as confirmed by his personal experience of its truth. "I am abundantly convinced, that our Heavenly Father does condescend to regard our approaches to Him for help in *our temporal affairs* as well as spiritual ones, and to calm the troubled soul. For I have in many instances proved His hearing and answering of prayer, and changing the storm into a wondrous calm. 'Trust in the Lord with all thy heart, and lean not to thy own understanding.'"

In 1849 he writes, "How do I desire for all my beloved family, that they, and we their parents, may be '*seeking first* the kingdom of God and His righteousness!' and then my faith is, that all things needful will be added to us. Mayst thou, my beloved child, be encouraged to a close walk with God; and the rich blessing of peace will be thy portion. Mayst thou know by blessed experience the God of Jacob to be thy refuge, under all the outward as well as inward conflicts of

G

time!—Nothing,—no, nothing at all,—can equal my fervent desires whilst writing, that thou mayst experience the blessing of true inward piety. Riches and honours, and all that this world can give thee, are as dross and loss compared to this in my estimation, and in my yearnings for thee."

The Friends at Kendal built their school by general subscription in 1770; Bryan Lancaster, one of their number, presenting the ground on which it stands. Many of the townspeople however shared in its advantages. Previously to 1815, it had been under the management of Jonathan Dalton, a brother of the well-known Dr. Dalton, who was himself at one time a tutor there. The boarding school, commenced by Samuel Marshall, though largely supported by Friends, was not limited to the children of members. Many boys were sent to it from Scotland, especially from Ayrshire. There were at one time 35 boarders in the house, besides as many day-scholars. The moral training inculcated truth-speaking and implicit obedience, and the great aim in teaching was *thoroughness*,—to lay a solid basis of sound instruction, on which a worthy superstructure might be raised. The motto before the eyes of the pupils on the wall of their school-room was the rule of the place: " Whatever is worth doing at all is worth doing well; and it is impossible to do anything well without attention." The master, as he himself on one occasion expressed it, " sought not to make brilliant, but useful characters." His familiar lectures on natural philosophy were much valued by his pupils, and tended to lead their attention to the study of first principles, — of cause and effect. From 1840 to 1845, Samuel Marshall took a useful share in the labours of the Friends' Educational Society.

But while diligent in his professional duties, he yet found time to take an active and leading part in various public institutions. Delighting to promote the spread of useful knowledge, he exerted himself in connection with the eminent Dr. Birkbeck, to establish as early as 1824 a Mechanics' Institute in Kendal, when there were only two others in the kingdom. He held the office of President for many years, and often delivered lectures on scientific subjects, which were highly appreciated. He united also in the formation of the Kendal Literary and Scientific Institute, was a Vice-President, and a Curator of their museum.

In his character as a citizen, he was for years elected Chairman of the Board of Guardians for the poor,—acted as Secretary to the Dispensary,

and manager of its funds,—was for a long time
the zealous Secretary of the Anti-Slavery Society,
—and filled the same office to the Peace Society.
He took an active interest in the British and
Foreign Bible Society, first as Secretary, then
Vice-President to the Kendal Auxiliary.

His meteorological researches and observations remain as a valuable contribution to science.
He had early formed acquaintance with John
Gough, "the blind philosopher," noted for his
surprising knowledge of botany, and whose observations on the rainfall and atmospheric changes
were begun in 1808, and continued by Dr. Dalton.
These were taken up by Samuel Marshall in 1823,
and carried on with diligence and accuracy till
the end of life, a period of 46 years. They are
carefully copied out in several volumes, and were
constantly given to the public in weekly and
monthly reports, as well as by an annual digest.

Nor was he less thorough in his religious
profession. From strong conscientious convic-
tions, he maintained a religious life and conversation as a member of the Society of Friends; whose
principles he firmly believed were founded on
Holy Scripture, and their practices in accordance
with its teaching and direction. During a time
of great religious unsettlement and separation, he

maintained his ground without swerving; but though many with whom he had united in worship for years, and who had grown up from youth to manhood under his eye, joined other religious communities, he retained their friendship and esteem, and rejoiced when he heard of their growth in grace, and their increased love and devotion to their Saviour.

In 1839, he gave up the boarding school, but continued to instruct day-scholars till 1855, when he retired from the scholastic profession, and was permitted to enjoy fourteen years of quiet retirement; relinquishing one object after another as his energies declined, and valuing the leisure thus afforded for communion with God, and preparation for the life to come.

On his retirement, a number of his former pupils presented him with a service of plate ; and at a breakfast given by them, they expressed in a written address their feelings of esteem and regard, for the share he had had in " forming their characters." In the strictness of his discipline, they discerned " the anxiety of a true friend,— one who looked to their ultimate welfare." After alluding to the pleasant remembrance and abiding results of his scientific lectures, they expressed a prayer, " that God might enable him, in the evening of life, to enjoy the continual sense of His presence, and in the end give him an abundant entrance into the everlasting kingdom of our Lord and Saviour Jesus Christ, through the merits of Him who died for us. We feel assured," they add, "that if thou hast one wish for thy pupils more than another, it is, that through faith in the Redeemer they may meet thee round the throne of God, washed in the same precious blood, and for all eternity enjoying the blessedness of Heaven." In his reply, he observed with marked humility, that "not possessing brilliant talents himself, he had not sought to make *brilliant* but *useful* characters. He had satisfaction in seeing many of them holding honourable positions in civil and religious society, and what was more, many who were he believed truly converted ; and he valued their heart-felt expressions, coming from men of mature years, who could look back with pleasure on his feeble endeavours to promote their improvement."

In the Tenth month of 1859, we find him writing in words of affectionate advice to a married daughter, after a long illness : — "Let not this season of trial be unimproved. Let thy Bible be the chief of thy reading. The treasures therein contained, will, by continual daily private reading, become more and more thy own. And though thou canst not actively attend to thy children according to thy wont, yet tender and earnest appeals to their young minds, will not be lost upon them, if they live. Thou wilt often, like many of us, be brought into discouragement by their untowardness, and under the feeling that thy precepts are of little if any use, since thou canst not see any evident fruit. Do not be weary and give up in despair; for in due season thou mayest reap, if thou faint not. I believe thy dear husband has been laying a good foundation, by his endeavours to store their minds and memories with Scriptural truths; and his success is evident to us all. Thy present condition is a very trying one in regard to thy family; but is it not more than probable, that it is one of the 'all things' that work together for good, when received as coming from the hands of a merciful Heavenly Father, who smites but to heal? Receive it as coming from Him, and the effect may prove one of thy greatest blessings."

Samuel Marshall was a much esteemed Elder in the Society of Friends, and was often constrained, in the fulness of Gospel love, to urge others with himself to increased watch-fulness and enquiry whether their hearts

were fixed on the only true foundation Christ
Jesus, through whose atonement and mediation
he looked for acceptance with his Heavenly
Father. Humility was a feature in his Christian
character, which increased the more, as he dwelt
on the long-suffering and wondrous love of God
towards his weak, rebellious creature, man. When
completing his 70th year in 1861, he writes,
" The Lord has been graciously pleased to own
my prostration of heart before Him, by the sensible manifestation of His goodness and mercy to
my soul."

As years passed on, he appears to have
dwelt much on our receiving the witness of the
Holy Spirit in the heart, that we are indeed
accepted of God in Christ. " And now, my
beloved," he writes in 1863, " how fares it with
thee in the highest sense? Dost thou *know* that
thy sins are forgiven, and blotted out by the
atoning sacrifice of the Son of God? Be convinced
that nothing less than the assurance of this, can
ever satisfy the longings and aspirations of the
immortal soul. High as the attainment is, it
will not be withheld, if earnestly sought for,
prayed for, and watched for. Do not rest satisfied
with any thing less than this ; then if the messenger on the pale horse come suddenly, he may be

no king of terrors to thee, but an angel of mercy.
O the deep, abiding peace that follows this assurance of reconciliation with God our Father, and
of Jesus being our Saviour and Redeemer!" Again
in the following year,—"it is a most blessed thing
to feel that our sins are forgiven, and blotted out,
for the sake and through the intercession of our
adorable Redeemer. And this must be attained
in this life; and we must never rest satisfied till
we have the evidence and assurance of it,—for
Christ said, 'if ye die in your sins, whither I go,
ye cannot come.' "

One characteristic of our dear Friend, was
his earnest desire to accomplish all that he felt
required of him as a religious duty. This led him
to be very diligent in visiting his Friends, especially those who were in any trouble or difficulty,
the sick or the sorrowful. He was in everything
very methodical, and even his visiting was systematic. He made a special point of calling on all
who were prevented from getting out to their meeting for worship. Many have spoken of the pleasure
and comfort they derived from his visits; and on
these occasions he sought, particularly of later
years, to bring constantly to view the priceless
blessings of the Gospel of Christ.

Hannah Marshall having a serious attack of

illness, the year 1867 closed in pensive reflections. 26th of Twelfth month. " I sit a deal with thy dear mother, and we have much religious conversation by ourselves. I trust both of us have an evidence, (though we would fain have it stronger,) that we have been enabled to put our whole trust in the pardoning mercy of God in Christ Jesus, our Saviour, our atonement, and our intercessor ; and are willing to wait in patience till we hear the summons, ' the Master is come, and calleth for thee.' "—31st of Twelfth month. " This has felt to me the most solemn day that I ever remember at the close of the year : with the certainty almost, that it will be the last to me and mother ;—but both of us are not so much con-cerned about the event, as we are that when the pale horse and his rider comes, we may be found having our lamps trimmed and burning ; and oil in our vessels also."

After a short season of renewed health, this beloved partner of his life was removed by death in the spring of 1868,—which proved a sore bereavement. For years she had been at times the object of his affectionate solicitude; but as her bodily strength diminished, her spiritual vigour increased, the nearer she approached the time of her departure. He greatly enjoyed sitting with her, recounting the goodness and mercy that had followed them all the days of their life, dwelling on the "*little while*" that would separate them from the united song of thanksgiving, in which they believed they should be permitted to join, to Him who they were assured would be with them to the end of life's journey. Very touching were the few broken words of praise he uttered, before leaving the room where he had watched her gentle departure, asking for himself, if consistent with the Divine will, as peaceful a dismissal. On conveying the mortal remains to their resting place, he bore testimony to that Almighty power which had supported her, giving her inexpressible peace, so that the chamber of death was as the gate of heaven.

During the succeeding months, he frequently said, " I mourn, but I do not murmur." His love for his children, and interest in their temporal and spiritual welfare, continued unabated : but he lived under the abiding sense that his days were numbered.

On the last return of his birth-day, he was much gratified by letters of remembrance from his children. In writing afterwards to one of them, referring to the occasion, he says :—" It would be ungrateful not to acknowledge the comfort they

gave me," and proceeds in a flow of thankfulness
to say, " I am often astonished at the state of
bodily health I am permitted to enjoy, though it
does diminish sensibly. But when I feel increasing feebleness, I am not surprised or distressed ;
especially when I see the mass of suffering around
me, and I free from acute pain : with so great an
amount of comfort at home, and so many truly
affectionate children and friends. Surely I may
say, why am I thus favoured? Not because I
have any deserts to plead. It was a day of
unusual searching of heart," he continues ;—
" and, humbled in the dust, I found that I had
not brought forth the fruits of a watchful heart ;
coming far short of my duty to God, my family
and my friends, as well as to my pupils in times
long past. But under the sense of my short-
comings, I was favoured to see, that I shall not
be forsaken by Him who has so mercifully followed
me through a long life. I am enabled at times to
believe and to *know*, that He will not desert me in
the short remainder of my days.

> ' His love in times past
> Forbids me to think,
> He'll leave me at last
> In trouble to sink.'

I desire to sit at His feet, and rest my whole soul

on His tender mercy and long-suffering : and
blessed be His name ! He is faithful to comfort
as well as to chasten ; for it is all in love—love
inexpressible."

As the anniversary of his wife's decease came
round, his thoughts constantly recurred to his
bereavement : but feeling the love of his Heavenly
Father renewed to him from time to time, he
believed he was, " through unmerited mercy,"
approaching the heavenly mansions, " assured of
an inheritance prepared for him " by the blessed
Saviour. " *Unmerited mercy !*" he would say in
his letters to one of his family, " as thy dear
mother used again and again to express it. * *
This love will have to be commemorated through
the endless ages of eternity. Then, and not till
then, can this amazing love be known and appreciated. I shall I trust be permitted to recognize
in those realms the ransomed and purified spirit
of my dearest earthly friend. No doubt thou
wilt think of her last hours on Seventh Day the
15th."

In the 7th month, Samuel Marshall suffered
from a fall, which it is thought proved the commencement of his last illness. Great debility
followed. " This attack," he says, " has introduced me into great searching of heart, to

H

ascertain where I am in the Divine sight; and I accept it as a decided call to be ready." * * * "Weak at times in faith," he writes a few days later, "I need to flee more and more to the only source of true consolation. There only is safety and an increase of strength to be found. There I am at times favoured to rest on the rock that can never be moved, so firm and stable is the foundation of the poor sinner's hope and trust and confidence. * * Debility is my chief ailment, I have no pain, and am (as I used to say to my dearest) *gently let down*. At times cheered with the light of my Heavenly Father's countenance, I could say to those around me, 'O magnify the Lord with me, and let us exalt His name together.'"

Five weeks after this, he still speaks of being free from pain, most of his faculties good, with a little failing of memory excepted, and adds, "What shall I render to the Lord for all His benefits? * * I never felt the true meaning of *unmerited mercy* so deeply as I have done, since it was so frequently the utterance of thy dear mother." And in the last letter addressed to any of his children, dated Tenth month 23rd, he says: "I often think of the general reticence of thy dear mother, in speaking of the world to come, or her own religious experience. But there are many sincere Christians who cannot speak of these things as others can, and yet exhibit undoubted evidence that they are deeply experienced. And is it not the better extreme of the two ? Christians feed on the 'hidden manna,' and have 'a white stone with a new name in it, which no man knoweth save he that receiveth it.' Would it not be better for some to talk less of their high confidence, and their wonderful ecstasies, before those who are weak in faith and conduct, and who are in danger of being depressed by comparison ? How assuredly do some speak of the *time* when they were enlightened or converted ! as if they could ascertain the period of the second birth as exactly as that of the first.* Might it not sometimes at least be better to speak of the fact with less decision, and always to consider the work not so much done, as doing ? or perhaps safer still, to pray that it might be done. So did David, ' Create in me a clean heart, O God, and renew a right spirit within me.' * * I could let my pen run on another half-hour, for my thoughts are in a very serious

* Though we are not prepared to say, that this can never be the experience of any, yet we must not insist on it as a universal mark of the true believer. Paul might so speak of his conversion, but not all the Apostles.

frame, musing on the uncertainty of time, and the future position of my dear children, and theirs. The sweet expressions of thy dear mother come before me with remarkable freshness. May we follow her, as she endeavoured to follow Christ! Then we may have good ground for hope that we shall meet with the same reward."

The following day, being First-day, the 24th of Tenth month, he addressed a letter of Christian feeling and advice, to two friends who were going abroad for the winter: and in the evening expressed a strong desire to go to meeting, as he believed he had a message for his friends. Soon after taking his seat, he rose and repeated the description of Christ at the last judgment from the 25th chapter of Matthew; then sat down exhausted: but on regaining his strength, commented on the two classes described, and the inevitable punishment of those who were not found on the right hand. To the boys of the Friends' School he addressed loving words of counsel and encouragement, and for all he manifested a deep feeling of Christian solicitude and love.

Next morning he was so poorly, that some of his children were sent for. The attack, though alarming, passed off; and on one of his daughters taking leave, he said, "I should like to tell thee as I told Jane yesterday, that I believe my sins are forgiven for the sake of my adorable Redeemer, unworthy as I feel myself to be. I wish to tell you, that if I am taken from you, you need have no anxiety on my account: all will be well."

On First-day, the 31st, he was seized with paralysis; and though conscious at times, was unable again to converse. But he enjoyed hearing Psalms and hymns, and repeated the 23rd Psalm as it was read to him, laying great emphasis on the last verse. On its being remarked, "Yes, dear father, goodness and mercy have indeed followed thee, and it will not be long before thou art dwelling in those blessed courts," he said, "Yes indeed, it is wonderful!" and at another time, "soon and for ever,—soon and for ever!" alluding to a favourite hymn. The sweet waiting frame of his spirit showed that his work was done, and that strength was given to support him in passing through the dark valley. Very little variation occurred till Fourth-day, the 3rd of Eleventh month: when he sensibly sank, and about half-past ten p.m., without sigh or struggle fell asleep in Jesus; his friends being fully persuaded, that as a shock of corn fully ripe, mellowed by the golden rays of the Sun of

Righteousness, he was borne rejoicing into the heavenly garner.

JOHN MARTIN,   67 28   1 mo. 1870
    Wellington, Somersetshire.

SILAS MARTIN,   71   8   4 mo. 1870
    Wellington, Somersetshire.

THOMAS MASON,   42 22   9 mo. 1869
    Melbourne, Australia.

MARY MILBOURNE,   60 29   6 mo. 1870
    Mountrath, Queen's County.

HENRY MOORHOUSE,   27 21   7 mo. 1870
    Leeds.   Son of Samuel and Jane Moorhouse.

Fraught with so much instruction to his friends were the closing days of this dear young man, that it is thought a brief record concerning him may suitably find a place in these pages.

Henry Moorhouse had his birth and education in our Society; was of a kind and unassuming disposition; and though of orderly walk, and a diligent attender of our meetings, yet seldom gave expression to feelings of a religious nature, until after the commencement of the illness which terminated his earthly course, and which was of little more than a week's duration. Though not of a robust constitution, he had never before been seriously ill.

In the early stages of this attack (remittent

fever) his friends did not apprehend anything serious as likely to result, the medical man speaking favourably of his case; but a day or two after taking his bed, Henry told his parents, he felt it best to inform them that he believed he should not recover. He knew it would be a heavy blow to them, but hoped they would be enabled to bear it. He then expressed himself to the following purport. During the previous night he had had a severe conflict of spirit. His sins, which were many, had been brought before him; but he had earnestly besought the Lord, through Jesus Christ, that he might be forgiven,—and he believed his prayers had been answered. He said he was not afraid to die, and felt that he could give all up. He, afterwards, in a comparatively calm and clear manner, gave directions relative to the settlement of his little outward concerns. Frequently, in the course of his illness, he prayed the Lord to prepare him for an admittance into His Heavenly kingdom, and often, during the intervals of relief from the fever, he appeared in a sweet and composed state of mind; though at other times he had his seasons of doubt and depression.

He was very desirous of seeing all his brothers and sisters, that he might take his leave of them : to whom, as it seemed called for, he was enabled to impart suitable counsel and advice, especially urging upon them the great importance of a thorough repentance in time of health. In sending messages of love to his other relatives, he also expressed concern for their spiritual welfare.

During the latter part of his illness he said, should it be the Lord's will to raise him up again, he felt he should live very differently ; but he did not expect to recover, and could not say that he desired it, except for the opportunity of living a better and more useful life. He said he was resigned in the Lord, whether for life or death. He manifested his thankfulness that he had never sought nor joined with evil company, but regretted that he had not devoted more time to the private reading of the Holy Scriptures. For some hours before the close, he was entirely unconscious : but he had previously given comforting evidence, that after having passed through much exercise of spirit he was prepared for the final change ; being enabled in humble confidence to express his belief, that for the sake of Jesus Christ his sins were forgiven, and that, through the Lord's redeeming mercy, he should be received into His kingdom.

WILLIAM MORLEY,   80 31 1 mo. 1870
 Woodbridge.
JOHN MORRISON, *Whitehaven.* 70 23 3 mo. 1870
EMILY MOUNSEY,   44 19 3 mo. 1869
 St. Leonard's-on-the-Sea. Wife of Edward
Mounsey, Denham, near Uxbridge. (Omitted
last year.)
MARY MOUNSEY, *Sunderland.* 75 9 9 mo. 1870
 An Elder. Widow of Thomas Mounsey.

She was the daughter of Jasper and Anne
Capper of Stoke Newington, near London. Of
her it may be said, that she possessed "the
ornament of a meek and quiet spirit:" and in
her comparatively youthful days she appears to
have known a true hunger and thirst after
righteousness; often retiring "to read the Bible
in private, and to seek for fresh supplies of
living water."

In the year 1817, she was united in marriage
to Thomas Mounsey of Sunderland; a union
which endured for thirty-three years, and which
was remarkably blessed; for both in temporal
and spiritual things, they were through their
married life one another's helpers and joy in
the Lord.

Her memoranda show, that having yielded
to the visitations of the Grace of God which

bringeth salvation, her desires were quickened after holiness, and a steadfast abiding in Christ Jesus; and under date 15th of Twelfth month, 1824, she writes:—" Had a sweet walk on the sands to-day alone, when I was tendered under a precious sense that 'my Beloved was mine, and I was His;' and that if this frail tabernacle were dissolved, my spirit would be prepared to unite with His who gave it. Having endured something of a spiritual fast for a few days past, it was very precious to me. How can I be sufficiently thankful for all His favours! The exercise of my soul has of late been, that I may indeed know a full surrender of all to Him, who can alone prepare His own sacrifice."

30th of Sixth month, 1826, she writes :— " I long to know a more complete living unto God, that His temple may be so fully established within me, as never to be clouded from my sight ; that I may be enabled to keep all earthly things in their right places, so that they may never for a moment intercept the heavenly vision. O may I be enabled to endure all those purifying baptisms, which are necessary to bring me into this precious state of union with the Divine Spirit !"

Her tender concern for the religious training of her children was deep and abiding. Their advancement in true godliness, and in the knowledge of our Lord and Saviour Jesus Christ, was the subject of her constant prayers; even that they might choose the Lord for their portion. Thus on the 19th of Sixth month, 1834, she observes, " I long to see the spiritual work begun in them, from a deep conviction of their need of a Saviour, and of the necessity of loving and obeying Him through their time of probation."

8th of First month, 1835. " In my evening retirement, my desires after living in a state of constant waiting were fervent, and remained lively for some time afterwards;—which is a favour." Again on the 18th she writes:—" I remembered that to-morrow is my birth-day for forty: a most important time of life, one that calls for the utmost vigilance and diligence, and the greatest care in yielding prompt obedience to all the requirings of the Great Head of the Church. In recurring to my state last year at this time, I hope I am not deceiving myself in thinking that a little ground has been gained, and that I have profited by some painful lessons. Oh! may He who has hitherto conducted me, continue to keep the city of my heart; for unless He do, my watching must be vain."

1st of Third month, 1835. " I have remembered afresh this evening in our silence after reading, that in the ' low valley ' there is the greatest safety; and my desire is (referring to a permanent change of residence) that no external changes may be suffered, in any degree, to prevent my earnest pursuit after that union of spirit with the Divine Spirit, which is the only joy worth pressing after in this life."   And again she observes, " I think I do desire above all things, that I may be enabled to endure all that is needful to bring me, in this life, into a capacity to live before the Lord in continual worship."

81st of Seventh month, 1836.   " My morning retirement was blessed with true desires after living wholly to the Lord : which however is not so much my case at present as I have formerly known, and which must be striven after.   Oh ! how does affliction drive one to His feet ! but why should the soul wait for this scourge, to be *driven* to that which can alone yield true comfort ?"

In another memorandum she tells us, " I was a little refreshed by reading the xv. chapter of 1 Corinthians, where the Apostle says, ' Thanks be to God which giveth us the victory through our Lord Jesus Christ.'   I want to feel a continual pressing after it, that I may not fall into the loathsome state of lukewarmness.

It is a dreadful state! one which I experienced most sorrowfully six or seven years ago: and I desire to suffer any affliction, rather than to be in such a state,—persuading myself that I was desirous of serving the Lord, and yet allowing my mind to go further and further into the things of time."

Writing to a relation who was undergoing much pecuniary trial, she remarks,—" I am comforted in the belief, that even these difficulties which of necessity cause anxiety, do not, when rightly submitted to, impede our spiritual progress. How all things else sink in importance, before the only object worthy of our pursuit—a preparation for our admittance into a state of unceasing worship, adoration, and praise, which should through Infinite love and mercy be begun in this life."

15th of Eleventh month, 1836. "Having been drowsy twice in my evening retirement, I felt disposed to omit it: but in withdrawing, was sweetly rewarded with an unusual degree of the spirit of supplication for myself and my immediate family, which strengthened my faith. I have indeed had to feel of late, that of ourselves we can do nothing; but how sweet it is to feel, that we have access to our Heavenly Father, so as

I

livingly to adopt the language, 'I know that Thou hearest me ,'—which was preciously the case this evening."

8th of Eleventh month, 1847. " I have been afresh stimulated to a degree of diligence which I know is greatly needed ; being, I fear, far from that state of continual watchfulness which is essential to the spiritual life. I long again to experience a living unto the Lord ; continually breathing unto Him, with the desire to serve Him in every thing,—in thought, word, and deed."

On the 7th of Twelfth month, 1850, she was deprived by death of the sweet companionship of her beloved husband. [See an account of Thomas Mounsey in the *Annual Monitor* for 1852.] Respecting her irreparable loss she writes,—" I cannot describe the state of my mind after this awful moment, when ' it pleased the Lord by death to separate us,' as to the body. [Still I believe] when it shall please the same Infinitely Wise Disposer of life and death to take me also, I shall for ever unite [with my beloved one] in celebrating His praise, who in His love and mercy prepared us to pass through this life together, for each other's benefit and happiness. In Him I have been enabled sweetly to trust, and have been graciously helped through all, to my own admiration."

5th of Sixth month, 1853, she writes, " I am in a dull state just now. I have great need to apply myself to the best and only remedy, continual prayer." In the evening of the same day she observes : " Since writing the above, I have felt afresh stimulated to press after that pure spring, which the blessed Saviour promised should be ' a well of water springing up into everlasting life,' in all those to whom He gives to drink of it ; and I may add, in whom the thirst for it continues. So assuredly I need not fear whilst a thirst for it is known ; only I would be in that state, that my spiritual ear might be ever ready to hear His holy commands ; and much do I long, that the remainder of my days may be spent in the fulfilment of His will concerning me. Then whenever the summons comes, it cannot find me unprepared : and whether enabled through His Grace to meet it with holy joy, or whether through the infirmity of the flesh nothing but quiet acquiescence is felt, all will be well, and my precious children I trust will be consoled. How comforting will be the belief that their dear parents are re-united for ever, in and through the Saviour, in His Kingdom, where there is no more

sorrow nor sighing, and all tears are wiped away !
May they and their little ones all join us in one
holy family above !"

For many months before her decease, she
was confined by declining health to her apart-
ment, but continued cheerful and resigned to the
last. On the 14th of Eleventh month, 1869, a
friend calling to see her, and expressing a hope
that she might before long be better, and able to
go out again, she said, " She must leave this :
she had rather it might not be so ; but she was
quite satisfied either way."

Her illness increasing, she several times
prayed aloud " that the Lord would sustain her
in this great affliction, and enable her to seek
help from Him unto the end." To one who
expressed the hope that she *did* feel sustained,
she said, " Yes ; I hope so ; indeed it would be
wrong to doubt it :" and to another who remarked
that " he believed all would be well with her,"
she warmly responded in the words of the hymn,

" Soon and for ever, the breaking of day
Shall chase all the night clouds of sorrow away."

During the last few weeks of her illness,
great weakness precluded much expression on
her part: but the same meek and quiet spirit
which had characterized her through life, con-

tinued to the close, when she peacefully fell
asleep in Jesus.

MARY NANKWELL,   77 6 11 mo. 1869
 Truro.

JOHN EDWARD NEALE, 10¼ 23 12 mo. 1869
 Clontarf, Dublin. Son of Nathaniel Neale,
 late of Carlow.

MARY NEILD,   60 30 3 mo. 1870
 Dean, near Charlbury. A Minister. Wife of
 Ralph Neild.

MARY PRISCILLA NEWMAN, 57 19 6 mo. 1870
 Buckfield, Leominster. Wife of Josiah Newman.

MARY ANN NIXON, 58 1 9 mo. 1870
 York, formerly Croydon.

MARGARET HELEN NORRIS, 1 6 5 mo. 1870
 Berkhamstead. Daughter of Daniel (Jr.) and
 Mary Helen Norris.

RICHARD NOWELL, *York.* 47 6 4 mo. 1870

SARAH OSMOND,   62 23 6 mo. 1870
 Clevedon, Somersetshire. Wife of Francis
 Osmond.

RACHEL OUTHWAITE, 67 24 11 mo. 1869
 Darlington. Widow of John Outhwaite.

ELIZABETH PACE,   58 15 6 mo. 1870
 Upper Clapton, London. Wife of Edmund
 Pace.

SARAH PALMER,   73 3   2 mo. 1870
  Gloucester.   Wife of James Palmer.

WALTER PEARMAN,   21 27   3 mo. 1870
  Wallingford.   Son   of   Alfred   and   Mary
  Pearman.

BERTRAM FELL PEASE,   1¼   2   3 mo. 1870
  Darlington.   Son of Henry Fell and Elizabeth
  P. Pease.

SOPHIA PEASE,   68 6   8 mo. 1870
  Darlington.   A Minister.   Widow   of   John
  Pease.

The subject of this brief notice was so well
known and beloved by a wide circle of friends,
that we do not like to omit from the pages of this
volume, a few particulars concerning one whose
life bore witness to her love to Christ, and dedication to her Master's cause. It is to be regretted
that she has left no memoranda from which any
extracts can be made, referring to her spiritual
growth, or the gradual preparation experienced
for service, whether in the ministry of the Gospel,
or in more private labour for the benefit of others.
A sense of her own unworthiness induced her
often to express the desire, that little might be
said about anything she had done,—so small she
felt it, compared with what had been done for
her ; and the remembrance of this wish must be

borne in mind, should any regret the limited character of this Memoir.

Sophia Pease was the youngest child of Joseph and Grace Jowitt of Leeds; and was born in 1801. Her father dying when she was very young, the care of a large family devolved upon her mother; whose Christian example, and interest for her children and others, were often recurred to with thankfulness. Several years were spent at boarding schools; and after returning home she frequently paid long visits to a married sister to whom she was deeply attached. Amid much in this happy home, that was gratifying to her lively and social disposition, she was often sensible of the restraining influence of the Holy Spirit: and in after life frequently acknowledged it had preserved her, amid temptations incident to association with a large and varied circle of acquaintance; enabling her to maintain a watchful and prayerful life. When about eighteen years of age, the death of an infant nephew whom she tenderly nursed was, we believe, the means of deepening her religious impressions, and causing a fuller dedication to the Saviour, whom from childhood she had loved.

In the year 1823, she was united in marriage to John Pease of Darlington, a union entered

upon after earnestly seeking for Heavenly gùid-
ance. During forty-five years they were permitted
largely to partake of the Divine blessing, and
were made eminently helpful to each other in
spiritual experience, and service for their Lord.
In her new allotment, she entered with affectionate
interest into the many demands upon her
sympathy and kindness, which a large circle
of relatives and friends could not fail to bring :
and having considerable leisure, she devoted it to
the claims of the poor, and to those who, from
sickness or trial, appeared to need her visits of
Christian love. Many of these visits we believe
were made a means of blessing to others, and
brought strength and refreshment to her own
soul.

In the year 1825 she first spoke as a Minister
in our meetings, and was recorded by Darlington
Monthly Meeting in 1834. During the earlier
years of her married life, she accompanied her
beloved husband on several of his religious
journeys; and in many cases shared with him
the labour and the reward of peace which was
often granted. Amongst their visits of Gospel
love may be named a residence of several months
in Ireland in 1834, which was often recurred to
as a time of especial interest; and many friend-

ships then formed were valued till the close of
life. In 1849 she paid a visit to the families in
Manchester meeting, accompanied by her valued
father-in-law Edward Pease; a labour of love,
which introduced her into deep feeling. Her
other engagements as a Minister were chiefly
confined to the members of her own Quarterly
Meeting.

Not unfrequently was she called to part with
her husband for religious service; and though
often for protracted periods, and at great personal
sacrifice, the cheerfulness with which she encouraged him to pursue the path of duty was very
instructive. In reference to his long absence
in America, she wrote many years afterwards
to one who was anticipating a like separation:
"Those have little need to fear, who commit themselves in child-like dependence upon our gracious
Heavenly Father. He who has cared for them
all their lives long, will surely be near to them,
when they are more decidedly proving their love
and allegiance to Him;—and how very strikingly
we have seen evidences of this care! Thou hast
my very tender sympathy. I desire never to
forget the mercy and loving kindness, which
watched over me and mine under similar circumstances, all unworthy as I am; though the

waves and billows are not forgotten, yet the faithfulness of our God is still a theme for gratitude and praise, as I love to dwell upon his tender care."

The following brief extracts from other letters will serve to show the thankful and trustful spirit in which she endeavoured to live ; and her desire that others, especially the young, might give their hearts to God.

"East Mount, Second month 1st, 1854. Much of sorrow and sickness seems abroad, and I desire daily to feel the privilege of meeting again in health at our breakfast table ; and truly we may say,

'Not more than others we deserve,
Yet God has given us more.'

To feel amid the varied trials and temptations of our day, that our witness is in heaven, our record is on high, has a sustaining, settling, and vivifying effect upon the mind, which it is the Christian's privilege to feel ; and then we may realize and experience the fulfilment of the assurance of our dear Saviour's words, ' Ask and ye shall receive,' —' Seek and ye shall find;'—and feel Him to be the bread of life, nourishing the soul."

East Mount, Eleventh month 7th, 1864. " How I would wish to encourage those in earlier life to devote the *best* of their time, strength, and all that they have lent to them, to their God and Saviour! and now I often wish more unreserved dedication had been mine: it is I believe good for us to feel in all its force,

> 'Nothing in my hand I bring,
> Simply to Thy cross I cling.'"

As years passed on, the unnumbered blessings of which she was partaker were constantly remembered, with feelings of deep thankfulness; and whilst bearing in mind the uncertainty of the future, she was ever anxious that the many proofs of her Heavenly Father's love might stimulate to greater diligence in the performance of her daily duties. At the commencement of 1868, she writes: "The close of the year, and opening of a new one, always brings with it pressing engagements; yet amid all these I trust we have had time for some of the solemn meditations, which in a review of the past, and the deep uncertainties as well as responsibilities of the future, should take possession of every Christian mind."

In the Seventh month of this year (1868,) she was unexpectedly called to part with her beloved husband. Under this sore bereavement she was remarkably sustained by her Saviour's presence; and during the remainder of her life, loved to meditate upon the happiness of which he was a partaker, remarkably realizing in her sorrow the truth of the words, "My grace is sufficient for thee." Casting her care upon the Lord, she was helped and comforted in a way almost surprising to herself. The following extracts are from letters written soon after his death. * * * "Mercy continues to be over all : while nature is daily more alive to the depth and varied character of the blank in our very united home circle. How good the Lord is, to grant that the spirit of my precious one should be so ever present, and over us ! * * * I am so unworthy of such love and tender care, that I am greatly humbled by it, and would strive to bless the Lord; for He hath done it. I love to sit and muse on the dealings of the Lord with His devoted servant, and of the hour in which, in boundless mercy to him, He took him to Himself to unite in the endless song."

And again, "all is mercy as regards our precious one, and the dealings of our most gracious God with him. The more we meditate upon them, the more evident they are ; reminding us of the text, ' Surely goodness and mercy have followed me all the days of my life, and I shall dwell in the house of the Lord for ever.' We must believe this mercy and love will be near us, and help be given according to our need; but the depths of a widow's heart must be felt to be understood. I thought I knew more about it, as I have often striven to lay myself along side many a proved one."

During the two years which elapsed from the time of her bereavement to the close of life, she felt called only to services of a more private character; but having tasted of affliction, was able to feel with others who were passing through deep waters; anxiously seeking to sympathize with them, and as opportunity offered to encourage them to trust in Him, whom she had proved to be "a covert from the storm." Many were the calls paid in her own meeting, in which she evinced her Christian love and interest for her friends; and it was instructive to observe her cheerfulness, and earnest desire that her sorrow should not prevent her from entering into the pleasures and happiness of those around her. The claims of the sick poor were not forgotten; and a cottage hospital, in which she had taken an active part from its commencement, received a large share of attention. Not a few conversations with its inmates were we believe fraught with lasting blessing.

K

Her health during the last few years had been frequently interrupted, and the difficulty of breathing alluded to in the following letter gradually increased; but it was borne with such cheerful patience, that those beyond her own family were little aware of its extent, or the effort often made not to let it interfere with duty.

To a near relative she writes : First month 6th, 1870. "I have not been quite so well latterly, my breathing more uncomfortable, but have no doubt it is all for the best to be thus disciplined. For amid all my deep sorrow, I have much around me to love and interest, and I might not bear in mind, so continually as I have done latterly, the uncertainty of everything to me. I have loved to trace my Heavenly Father's hand with me from youth upward ;—how in very faithfulness He has dealt out His blessing in sorrow, suffering and bereavement ; yet how His love has felt as a canopy when in my deepest sorrow :—and then of joys surely I have had a large share ; so that I desire to bless and praise His name, and my earnest prayer is that in nothing I may grieve His Holy Spirit ; for great is the need of constant watchfulness."

Soon after this time other symptoms caused considerable anxiety to her relatives, but they did not prevent her taking an active part in her usual avocations, until about six weeks before her death; which were spent entirely upstairs. Allusion being made to the brightness which she was remarkably permitted to maintain during this time, she replied: " I wish to do what is right in this and all other things; but if what I believe and what I say is true, to go to heaven— such a bright place—how can I be gloomy?" and these words fitly express the state of her mind in the prospect of death—and amid much bodily weakness, there never seemed any doubt in reference to the unseen, which is eternal.

She was mercifully preserved from suffering, saying on more than one occasion: " I have no pain. God seems to have taken away all my aches and pains, and cast them on my Saviour." She often dwelt upon the absence of all condemnation, not on account of anything she had done, for she felt *she* had done nothing; but because Christ had done everything for her, and had Himself taken away all her sins:—that this was the more remarkable, when she remembered how often she had resisted the strivings of the Holy Spirit; saying how she longed that all her friends might realize Jesus as their Saviour, and having found Him, be enabled to bring others to Him also.

She alluded to the loss sustained by all, in not more frequently communing with each other on their faith and hope; quoting the words, " Then they that feared the Lord spake often one to another," &c.—and to all with whom she was brought in contact, she would speak of His lovingkindness to her all her life long; saying in reference to her own experience, and for those dear to her,

" He who has helped thee hitherto,
Will help thee all thy journey through."

She sought to impress on her attendants the reality of religion, that it *is* the power of God unto salvation, and spoke to them of the wondrous nature of His condescension to poor, finite man : how all, both great and small, are called upon to praise Him. "Yes," she would say, " the *small* shall praise Thee."

Many are the precious promises of the Gospel which she emphatically repeated : " Ask and ye shall receive, seek and ye shall find." * * " I am the resurrection and the life." "Blessed is the man that maketh the Lord his trust ; his leaf shall not wither, and whatsoever he doeth shall prosper." * * " I will praise the Lord at all times : His praise shall continually be in my mouth." Very near the close she said, "Farewell, all is peace you know, all is comfort, all is joy : " and shortly after, " He reigns God over all." These were nearly the last words she spoke. Gently did the spirit leave its tabernacle, to join her beloved in the unclouded presence of her Saviour and her God.

> " Oh, call it not death ! it is life begun,—
> For the waters are passed, the home is won ;
> The ransomed spirit hath reached the shore,
> Where they weep and suffer and sin no more :
> She is safe in her Father's house above,
> In the place prepared by her Saviour's love.
> To depart from a world of sin and strife,
> And to be with Jesus,—yes, this is life."

CHARLES PECKOVER, 71 4 5 mo. 1870
Thornton Heath, near Croydon.

MARTHA PHILLIPS, 74 26 4 mo. 1870
Reading. Widow of William Phillips.

LAMBERT PIDWELL, *Truro.* 80 3 8 mo. 1870

ALICE PIM, 8½ 15 12 mo. 1869
Monkstown, Dublin. Daughter of Frederick W. and Hannah Pim.

SUSAN PIM, 11 21 6 mo. 1870
Wicklow. Daughter of Joseph and Lydia Pim.

ISABELLA SOPHIA PIM, 47 9 8 mo. 1870
Glenayeragh House, Monkstown. Wife of Thomas Pim.

DANIEL POTTER,   78 28   5 mo. 1870
  Layer Breton, Essex.
HANNAH PRITCHARD,   71   9 10 mo. 1870
  Birmingham.
WILLIAM PRYER, *Tottenham.* 82   5   8 mo. 1870
THOMAS RATHBONE,   53 15   8 mo. 1870
  Hartshill in Warwickshire.

Born a Friend, he outlived every other member of the little meeting at Hartshill; and did not associate himself with any other body of Christians, until after he had sat solitarily for several months without a prospect of companionship. The ancient Meeting-house, built in 1720, and only two miles from the village where George Fox was born, was accordingly closed, and remained so for thirty years. Some years ago however, through the instrumentality of the late Edward Brewin and others, the building was cleared of rubbish, and made available for public meetings. The people rejoiced in this, and none more so than Thomas Rathbone. The master of an endowed school close by dying about this time, the Trustees all agreed to look out for a Friend as his successor, and having succeeded in finding one, the meetings have been restored and held weekly. The numbers who attend on First-day morning range from twelve to twenty persons, and in the evening from thirty to fifty. A Friend writing last Twelfth month says, "some of the attenders went to no place of worship previously, and we believe a good work is going forward. Jesus is preached, and to Him the people are directed as their Teacher."

Thomas Rathbone, who never lost his interest in the Society, was made happy in his last days by this resuscitation of Hartshill Meeting, which he regularly attended, and by his will desired to be laid in the burial-ground adjoining. This was done on the 19th of Eighth month, and a solemn meeting was held on the occasion, attended by a considerable number of his neighbours, and by some Friends from a distance.

FRANCES REEVES,   84   8 10 mo. 1869
  Grand Parade, Cork.   Widow of John Reeves.

LUCY EMMA RENISON,   2   9   8 mo. 1870
  Everton, Liverpool. Daughter of James and
  Mary Ann Renison.

SUSAN JANE REYNOLDS,   27 27 10 mo. 1869
  Devonshire Square, London. Died at Bournemouth.

JOSEPH STRANGMAN RICHARDSON,
  Tramore.   54 28   4 mo. 1870

SARAH RICHARDSON,   62 13   5 mo. 1870
  Snow's Green, Shotley Bridge.

JANE ROBSON,   1¼   4   9 mo. 1870
   Dalton, Huddersfield.   Daughter of Joshua
William and Elizabeth Robson.

THOMAS ROBINSON, *Kendal.*   76 28 10 mo. 1869

WILLIAM BREAREY ROBINSON, 1 21   1 mo. 1870
   Croydon.   Son of William and Mary Ann
Robinson.

ELEANOR ROBINSON,   59   9   5 mo. 1870
   Calder Bridge, near Garstang.

JOHN ROGERS,   72   8   6 mo. 1870
   Bessbrook, near Newry.

SARAH ROWNTREE,   72 16   4 mo. 1870
   Bradford in Yorkshire.   Widow of Isaac
Rowntree.

MARY SEED,   78 29   5 mo. 1870
   Manchester

ROBERT HILL SERGEANT,   59 21   1 mo. 1870
   Birmingham.

HENRY SESSIONS,   25 18 11 mo. 1869
   Cardiff.   Son of Jesse and Eliza Sessions of
Gloucester.

EDWARD SEWELL, *Hitchin.*   79 13   8 mo. 1870

THOMAS SHARPE,   70 22   4 mo. 1870
   Howgill, near Sedbergh.   An Overseer, of
whom it is testified, that " he was a good
man, and died in the faith and hope of the
glorious Gospel of the blessed God."

ROBERT SHAW, 73 5 6 mo. 1870
Upper Rathmines, Dublin.

MATILDA SHEPPARD, 66 15 11 mo. 1869
Hemel Hempstead. Widow of William
Sheppard.

ALFRED SHEPPARD, 82 14 12 mo. 1869
Hemel Hempstead. Son of the above.

MARY ISABELLA SHERWOOD, 67 27 12 mo. 1869
Halifax. Widow of Thomas Sherwood of Hull.

ANN SHIELD, 54 22 4 mo. 1870
Bristol. Wife of William Shield.

HENRY ELLIS SHIPLEY, 1½ 12 4 mo. 1870
Bristol. Son of Alfred and Sarah Ann Shipley.

MARIA SIMMS, 44 8 7 mo. 1870
Chipping Norton, Oxon. Wife of Charles Price
Simms. The decease of this dear friend took
place after an illness of about three days, which
were passed mostly in a state of unconsciousness. She was an exemplary wife and mother,
and much beloved by her family and friends :
who are consoled in believing that their loss is
her eternal gain.

ALBERT ISAAC SIMMONS, 81 24 2 mo. 1870
London. Son of Ebenezer L. Simmons.

SYLVANUS SMEE, 34 23 2 mo. 1870
Stamford Hill, London. Son of the late
William and Margaret Smee.

LYDIA SMITH,   63 15 10 mo. 1869
  Manchester.   Died at Leeds.
ROSAMOND SMITH,   33 20 2 mo. 1870
  Rockhampton in Queensland.   Daughter of
  Lister and Deborah Smith of Bocking, Essex.
TILL ADAM SMITH,   50 17 5 mo. 1870
  Weston-super-Mare.
LEONARD SNOWDEN,   55 11 1 mo. 1870
  Accrington.
ELIZABETH SOUTHALL,   67 26 2 mo. 1870
  Southport.   Wife of Richard H. Southall.

This dear Friend bore a long and suffering illness with much patience. Some weeks previous
to her removal, though in deep self-abasement, she
remarked to her sorrowing husband, "I am not
afraid to die." She had long felt her need of a
Saviour, and fully accepted the great Scriptural
truth "that God was in Christ reconciling the
world unto Himself." In this Almighty Saviour
she was enabled to put her whole trust, fully
realizing also the necessity of the cleansing and
disciplinary operations of the Holy Spirit in her
heart, that the all-important work of sanctification
might go forward.

ANN SOUTHAN, *Manchester.*   68 16 5 mo. 1870
JACOB SPARROW,   52 23 9 mo. 1870
  Fox Rock, Dublin.

For many years of his life this dear Friend exhibited the fruits of a living faith in Christ, by a constant endeavour "to do justly, to love mercy, and to walk humbly with his God." A kind consideration for the poor was a marked feature of his character. By them he was much beloved, and has left a lasting memorial in the hearts of many; in him the orphan found a friend and counsellor, and on his head the blessing of the widow and the desolate ones was often invoked.

On one occasion, having been betrayed into some hastiness of temper when appealed to by a poor woman for assistance, he records in his memoranda that it occasioned him much regret, that he asked her forgiveness, and entreated his Heavenly Father to preserve him from yielding to a similar temptation in future;—adding, it is much better to bear with the complainings of the poor, than to say one word which might increase their sufferings.

He ever took a humble view of his own religious attainments, esteeming others better than himself; and in works of private benevolence was careful not to let his left hand know what his right hand was doing.

In business transactions he was most particular to do what he believed to be right, although his scrupulous conscientiousness might sometimes involve considerable pecuniary loss. One day at Meeting, having heard a minister speak impressively on the desire evinced by so many to accumulate wealth, and of the danger incurred, whilst the mind is so engrossed, of burying our talents in the earth, he writes respecting it; "I hope what I have heard to-day may have the effect of loosening me from the things of earth. Although I feel no wish to accumulate wealth, and only desire to spend well what little the Almighty has blessed me with, yet I cannot help feeling that I am too much clogged with earthly cares, and that my heaven-ward progress is thereby retarded. I often long for an assurance that all may be well with me, if called away from earth. How delightful it must be to be able to rejoice in Christ our Saviour!"

On another occasion he thus records his feelings; " Soon after taking my seat in Meeting to-day, this passage of Scripture impressed my mind, 'Peace I leave with you, My peace I give unto you; not as the world giveth, give I unto you.' I felt forcibly how unsatisfying to the immortal soul is anything which *the world* calls peace, and how inestimably precious is that peace which is obtained through Christ our Saviour."

Those who knew him best feel an humble trust, that He who raised this desire in his heart, was pleased to bless his longing soul with joy and peace in believing. His last illness was unexpected and short, during part of which his mind wandered a little; but a few of his expressions, uttered in clearer intervals, evinced that he had no fear, and that he felt he was going to the God and Saviour whom he loved, and had humbly endeavoured to serve.

His sorrowing friends, while deeply lamenting their great loss, can, nevertheless, thankfully acknowledge the comfort they feel in the happy assurance vouchsafed to them, that through the atoning sacrifice of the Lamb of God, who taketh away the sin of the world, their beloved one has been admitted into that city whose walls are salvation, and whose gates are praise.

THOMAS STEACEY, *Waterford.* 83 18 10 mo. 1869

WILLIAM STEPHENSON, 75 4 12 mo. 1869
 High Bentham, near Lancaster.

THOMAS HANDCOCK STRANGMAN,
 Waterford. 69 21 12 mo. 1869

WILLIAM STURGE, 80 27 4 mo. 1870
 Chipping Sodbury in Gloucestershire.

L

JOSEPH WILLIAM TAYLOR,   10   2 11 mo. 1869
    Croydon.   Son of Joseph Taylor.
CAROLINE TAYLOR, *Cork.*   79 28   1 mo. 1870
WILLIAM THISTLETHWAITE,   56 28   1 mo. 1870
    The Uplands, Wilmslow.   A Minister.

To many of our readers the name and
general character of William Thistlethwaite will
be well known.   Springing from an obscure
corner of one of the Yorkshire dales, he was
nevertheless not born for himself alone, but
was led into paths of usefulness, in different
localities, which brought him in various ways
before the public.   He was gifted with no small
measure of intellectual and moral influence; and
in reviewing his course through life, we are
induced to believe, that He who bestowed on him
such talents, also provided the sphere in which
they should be employed.

        " God gives to every man
The virtue, temper, understanding, taste,
That lifts him into life,—and lets him fall
Just in the niche he was ordained to fill."—COWPER.

William Thistlethwaite was the third son of
Richard and Margaret Thistlethwaite, and was
born in 1813, in Widdale near Dent, in the West
Riding of the County of York, where his father
followed the occupation of a farmer.   When about

six or seven years old, his parents removed to the
the contiguous valley of Dent. Here, like most
country boys, he spent the years previous to going
to school between work and play:—rambling about
among the hills and dales of the neighbourhood,
or tending the sheep and cattle. He was however
docile and thoughtful beyond his years, and could
be relied on in the duties assigned him. The
activity and energy thus acquired, and the dispositions manifested, were indicative of the character
more fully developed in after life.

At nine years of age, he began to go to a
school at Lea Yeat, then under the charge of
John Alderson; but the distance being considerable, and the weather often unfavourable, his
attendance was irregular, and his progress small.
In the year 1825, he was sent to Ackworth
School, but remained in that Institution only two
years; his age, by the regulations then in force,
not admitting of his longer continuance. During
this period he made good progress, being quick
in his attainment of knowledge; and even in his
leisure hours studious, and fond of reading.

On his return from Ackworth, he was again
placed under some disadvantages; living in a
remote country district, with few desirable
companions, or opportunities favourable to the

acquisition of knowledge. But he enjoyed the high privilege of a sound moral and religious training. His parents were very solicitous and careful, that their children should be brought up " in the nurture and admonition of the Lord." The affectionate advice of a pious mother is often of the happiest influence, and this was not wanting, as he frequently acknowledged. A regular attendance of meetings for public worship was inculcated, both by precept and example. Such care and guidance may not always appear to produce the desired result, and even in some cases seem to be of no avail : yet *generally* the good becomes visible sooner or later : sometimes early, and at other times " after many days." Under this parental care, in the instance before us, he was preserved from hurtful companionships, which often afterwards excited his gratitude and thankfulness. He was also privileged, when leaving his father's roof, to be under the care of a dear Friend, a relative, well qualified to foster what was good, and repress anything of a contrary tendency : and this not so much by direct command, as by the force of example, and the influence of a truly Christian character.

His father, thinking it best to put out his son to some handicraft business, placed him in

1828 under James Thistlethwaite, clogger and leather cutter, at Bainbridge in Wensleydale. This however was not the avocation of the youth's own choice, but he worked at it assiduously, and was quick at learning the trade; though he never liked it, and was not disposed to continue in it. Under these circumstances, he lost no opportunity of improving his mind, in order to prepare himself for a change of employment, if any opening presented itself. Meanwhile his hearty good nature, and his ability, gained him many friends, both amongst young and old; and, among those of his age, there were few whose services in the promotion of public objects in the district, were more sought after. He was warmly interested in the Temperance cause, and employed himself in advocating it throughout the neighbourhood; and in conjunction with other young men, was active in supporting local agencies set on foot for their mutual improvement. It is still remembered by a Friend, how that when William was about seventeen or eighteen years of age, he was found earnestly discussing with his employer passages in " Doddridge's Rise and Progress of Religion in the soul." He became fond of metaphysical enquiries, and one of his favourite books was *Paley's Moral and Political Philosophy,* which, though rather bulky, he carried about under his buttoned coat, to refer to in spare moments.

His master seeing the bent of his mind encouraged him, and before long wrote to his father to say, that he thought his son was qualified for something better, both for himself and for others, than to be " a mere hewer of wood or a cutter of leather,"—offering also to give up any claim he himself had by their agreement, if opportunity should occur of his entering on a more promising sphere. Soon after, a teacher was wanted for a small school at Counterside, near Bainbridge : the situation was offered him ; and, though continuing to reside with his late master, he now entered on the profession which was to be the main business of his life. He engaged in it with zeal and ardour, as being an employment after his own heart, and feeling the importance and responsibility of his calling.

He conducted the school at Counterside to general satisfaction till 1834. His scholastic attainments at that period could not be large, but he had an active and vigorous mind. His manner of teaching was lively and agreeable ; he had a love of children, which he retained to the end of life, and he took a warm interest in the progress of his pupils.

Endeavouring faithfully to instruct his scholars, he enriched and enlarged his own mental acquirements ; and in his efforts to elevate the character of those around him, he himself partook of the benefit: so that in more senses than one he found the words verified : " it is more blessed to give than to receive,"—" there is that scattereth, and yet increaseth,"—and " he that watereth, shall be watered also himself."

It may be thought that the time spent in the workshop at Bainbridge was to a certain extent wasted : and perhaps in a strictly business point of view it might be so. But an active and thoughtful mind, by being thrown on its own resources, is often strengthened and rendered the more independent ; and the guardianship of so good a master at this, the most impressible period of his life, can scarcely be over-estimated. James Thistlethwaite, his master, was a man of rare virtues : mild and humane in disposition, and scrupulously conscientious. Possessed of an intelligent mind, and unusually free from prejudice, he gave his ready assent and support to " whatsoever things are true, honest, pure, lovely, and of good report." And if his rule of life had been taken from these words of Paul to the Philippians, he could scarcely have illustrated them more faithfully than he did by his practice. Such influence in that retired situation, there can be little doubt, had a powerful effect in moulding the character of his youthful charge ; who, though he did not at that period speak much of his own spiritual experience, gave evidence that through the operation of the Holy Spirit, he was favoured to " grow in grace, and in the knowledge of our Lord and Saviour Jesus Christ."

At this juncture, the Society of Friends had their attention drawn to the educational wants of children belonging to the families of those, who were connected with them by descent, or as attenders of their religious meetings, but not in membership. A school for such had been established by the Friends in Yorkshire, and it was further intended to found a similar one at Penketh near Warrington, in South Lancashire. Both these institutions were designed to be of an industrial character, in which out-door farm labour or garden work for the boys, and domestic employments for the girls, should be largely combined with scholastic instruction.

William Thistlethwaite, though only twenty-one years of age, was induced to apply for the office of Master or Superintendent, and appeared, from the very circumstances we have detailed, to have special qualifications for the work. It was indeed to some degree a new experiment in education : but he entered upon it with all his energy of body and mind, and his labours were eminently successful. For twelve years he continued to preside over the institution, and diligently to advocate the advantages of the method on which it was conducted. In the proceedings of the Friends' Educational Society, (a useful and active association in the period referred to,) will be found two earnest reports or tractates on the Industrial system, from his pen ;—as well as other contributions. His style of teaching and views of education were original, and elicited general approval ; —though at the present day the amount of time given to industrial pursuits in the school at Penketh is considerably diminished.* By the responsibilities thus early devolving upon him, it is thought his youthful vivacity was in degree re-

* Similar schools to that at Penketh were opened by the Society of Friends at Ayton, Sibford, and Brookfield in Ireland : the late James Cropper established one under his own direction at Fearnhead, for Irish orphans ; Lady Byron and others in different parts of the country ; and the system is now adopted with marked advantage at some of the Reformatory Schools of the present time.

pressed; but his intellectual powers were largely developed, and his character acquired additional strength and maturity.

In 1846, he left Penketh, owing to changes in prospect, and for a while occupied the post of Master on Duty at Ackworth. But he had not been long there, before an offer was very unexpectedly made to him of the boarding school at Tulketh Hall near Preston; and after serious consideration he entered on the new undertaking, in company with his friend and future brother-in-law, Dr. Satterthwaite. In 1847 he married. The partners conducted the school at Tulketh for six years; but the lease expiring, they concluded to erect new school premises at Lindow Grove near Wilmslow, to which they removed in 1853.

In addition to the routine of a professional life extending over more than a quarter of a century, William Thistlethwaite was ever ready to take part in forwarding many of the public movements of the day;—in the work of the Bible Society, the Friends' Educational Society, the Manchester Friends' Institute, visiting schools, writing essays and lectures, &c. The productions of his pen were mostly intended for particular occasions; but in 1865 he published a small volume of

" Four Lectures on the Rise, Progress, and Past Proceedings of the Society of Friends,"— *a historical review*, as the author observes, *not a history*, of the period of which they treat.

While passing successively from one situation in life to another, our dear Friend was anxious to follow the pointings of duty. All views having reference to worldly advantage *merely*, were subordinated to the sense of what was required of him, in serving his Divine master, and becoming useful to his fellow-men. Often would he acknowledge, with a heart overflowing with gratitude, how marvellously he had been led in the pathway of life, and how many unmerited blessings had been showered down upon his head. He would own in humble thankfulness, that from the time when he was taken " from the sheep-cotes, from following the sheep," the Lord had been with him and round about him, " whithersoever he went."

Throughout these years, there was a manifest deepening of religious feeling in his mind : and this led him about the year 1860 to take steps for relinquishing the scholastic profession, with a view to the fuller devotion of his time and talents to the service of Christ. He retired to the house he had built near Wilmslow, and soon after felt himself called to speak as a Minister in our

Meetings for Worship.   In 1864 he was recorded
as a Minister.   He travelled very little beyond
the limits of his own Monthly Meeting except
by appointment, but frequently took occasion to
visit their smaller or more remote particular meetings.

He was at various times engaged in important services under the appointment of the
Yearly Meeting.   He was on the Committee for
visiting most of the counties in the West and
South-East of England, as well as Yorkshire.
In 1864 and 1865 he was also one of the
Committee that visited the Yearly Meeting of
Ireland; and it is believed was at all the meetings
of Friends in that country.   "On these occasions,"
says one who was united in these visits, "the
depth of his religious sympathies, his large-
heartedness, and the breadth and comprehensive-
ness of his views, gave an especial value to his
services.   His ministry was sound, weighty, and
impressive : and in meetings for discipline, or
those of a more social character, his remarks were
often peculiarly pertinent and instructive.   His
thoughts were generally original, and he never
lost his native independence of character : but
this was accompanied with an ever-deepening love
of the brethren, and an earnest endeavour to

maintain it unimpaired in the bond of peace. He enjoyed the companionship of the young; and many, we doubt not, can recur with thankfulness to his words of counsel or of cheer, strengthening and animating them in the heavenward path of duty."

In his own neighbourhood, the suavity and ease of his manner rendered him very accessible to all. His judgment was much relied on by men in his own position in life; and those less acquainted with the world, as well as the poor, found in him a kind friend and judicious adviser. Often would he extend a word of warning to tradesmen and others, whom he saw in danger of falling into temptation; and generally with beneficial effect. A few earnest, loving words, spoken with the freedom of a brother, often sank deep into the heart of the hearers, and it is believed were blessed to them.

But duty to God was the ruling motive in his heart, and earnest were his desires for the advancement of His kingdom on earth. Especially dear to him was the welfare of our own portion of the church, and much did he lament the divisions which it was his lot to witness in certain portions of it. For its welfare he was willing to spend and be spent, and even "not to

M

count his life dear to himself, so that he might finish his course with joy." And truly, as the end unconsciously drew near, his mind seemed to glow with a radiance and a tenderness, which was felt, but cannot be expressed. During the last year of his life, there was an evident decay of physical power; but disease of the heart was not even suspected: nor until the last two months was it known to exist.

At an early period of his illness, on being made aware of its serious character, he said with deep feeling : " What I do thou knowest not now, but thou shalt know hereafter." Measures were taken for having his few unfinished worldly matters finally settled, and no anxieties remained. His wish to communicate with a few near relatives was granted ; and he sent words of affectionate encouragement to a dear invalid brother : " Be of good cheer, brother. We serve a good Master." Seeing his wife in tears, he said, " Don't grieve, dear ! that would be dishonouring God. My trust is firm and unshaken."

Though often unconscious from the force of the disease, various expressions used from time to time are remembered. To a friend who called to take leave of him, before setting out on a long journey, he expressed a feeling " that we had suffered loss, for want of freer communion on subjects of deepest interest." To a young relative he said, " Keep humble, dear ! especially as regards intellectual attainments. I have had of late such views of humility as I cannot express."

Early on the 10th of First month, believing the crisis imminent, he begged his beloved partner not to leave him, saying : " Let us have our last hour of joy together: this is quite a little heaven." During the same day, his sister - in - law unexpectedly arrived ; and there were such evidences of joy at this visit, bearing as she did loving messages from her invalid husband, as were very affecting. He said to her, " I have, from the commencement of this illness, had given me such a sense of peace and joy, as I have greatly marvelled at. Indeed I have stood in doubt of myself, whether it was right : not a cloud ! not a cloud! It is wonderful."

Preserved from all doubts and fears, he calmly awaited the approach of death. " I cannot say much," he observed, " nor do I think it desirable." Amidst the rambling caused by the disorder affecting the brain, while rapidly flitting from one topic to another, verses from the Psalms would frequently intervene : " O satisfy us with

Thy mercy;" or, "I shall be satisfied, when I awake, with Thy likeness:"—mingled with interjaculatory prayer for others as well as for himself. In one of his moments of consciousness, he said emphatically: "The life of religion in the soul is what is most wanted in the present day."

He frequently expressed his firm reliance on the goodness and mercy of God through Jesus Christ, and his unwavering faith, that whether it pleased his Heavenly Father to make his life long or short in this world, "all would be well in the end." Love towards God and his Saviour appeared to pervade every aspiration; and the outflowings of his love to his fellow-men were scarcely less marked. The burden of his mind may be gathered from his words: "let all bitterness and wrath and anger cease," with other expressions of like import, again and again repeated.

Being told one day, that a body of Christian Friends in the neighbourhood had remembered him at their weekly prayer meeting, he said after a pause: "The will of the Lord be done." Once, after a period of partial rallying, he said: "It may be I must stay a little longer with you. HE knows best:" and turning to his wife he added,

" We see not yet the great mystery,—but we shall see it soon."

Part of the 23rd Psalm being repeated to him, he promptly added the rest, beginning " Thou anointest my head with oil,—my cup runneth over." As his weakness increased, he said, " O that I had wings like a dove! then would I fly away, and be at rest." And when the closing scene came, and he knew that death was at hand, in clear accents he uttered, to the abiding comfort of his surviving friends, the words " *All is well*," and entered into his everlasting rest.

GEORGE THOMAS,   78   7 12 mo. 1869
Bristol.   An Elder.

As this beloved Friend was extensively known and valued, both in our own Religious Society and beyond it, it seems due to his memory that some notice of him should find a place in this volume.

George Thomas was a member of our Society by birth ; and in mature life he evinced a conscientious attachment to the principles and practices of Friends. He was not in the habit of conversing much on religious subjects ; but as life advanced, it became increasingly evident that, whilst retaining an intelligent preference for

the arrangements of our own Society, he more
clearly saw, and more deeply felt, the paramount
importance of those fundamental truths of the
Gospel, which are regarded as such by Friends
in common with our fellow Christians of other
denominations.   During the later years of his
life, he evinced much sympathy, and was in the
practice of contributing with great liberality, to
the support of means for spreading the glad
tidings of the Gospel, both among the destitute
classes in our own country, and in heathen nations
abroad.   His pecuniary liberality in this respect
was not limited to the support of efforts made by
Friends, but extended freely to all, under whatever name, whom he regarded as among those
who love our Lord Jesus Christ in sincerity.

For many years he acceptably filled the
offices of Overseer and Elder, and in various
ways devoted much time and attention to the
affairs of our Religious Society.   In the year
1831 he was united in marriage to Elizabeth
Green, who survives him.   Through the long
period during which this union was permitted
to continue, it proved under the Divine blessing,
not only largely conducive to his own happiness,
but we believe not less so to his usefulness to
others.

Our dear friend possessed ample pecuniary means; and his income for an extended course of years, was *chiefly* devoted to the good of others. Liberality to the poor was a conspicuous feature of his character : but he was careful to exercise it with wise discrimination ; and when needful he did not shrink from taking much trouble, in order to ascertain in what way his help might be most effectually given. He was one of the founders of the Bristol General Hospital, and to the end of his life he continued to watch carefully over the affairs of that Institution, and to contribute largely to its support.

He possessed, in no common degree, the confidence and esteem of his fellow-citizens, his judgment being often consulted and his aid sought in important matters, whether of a local character, or embracing a wider range of public or political interest. For many years he filled the important office of Chairman to the Bristol Charity Trustees, giving to the duties devolving on him in this responsible position much of his time, as well as persevering and even minute attention. The Christian simplicity and undeviating integrity of his character,—his sound judgment and practical sagacity,—and the kindness and courtesy of his manner towards all, won for him the esteem of all classes. And though possessing a disposition remarkably free from any tinge of ambitious feeling, he enjoyed a place and influence among his fellow-citizens, which has not often been possessed in the same degree by a private individual. This was remarkably shown at his funeral, which was attended by clergymen of the Established Church, and Dissenting ministers of all denominations, as well as by numerous representatives of the Corporation, and other public bodies in the city. Indeed, the manifestations of sympathy and respect throughout the city on this solemn occasion were so general, as to give to it much of the appearance of a public funeral.

Among other benevolent and philanthropic enterprises, George Thomas felt a lively interest in the Temperance cause. He gave up the use of all intoxicating beverages more than thirty years ago: and whilst advocating such abstinence on moral and religious grounds, he not unfrequently referred to the improvement in his own health, which had followed his giving up the use of wine, and drinking water only. He generously contributed, during many years, to the funds required for the Temperance operations in the West of England: and at his death he bequeathed £2000 to the Bristol Temperance Society.

The large extent to which, during many years of his life, our beloved friend was occupied with engagements of a more public character, was not allowed to weaken his interest in the affairs of our own Religious Society. He was a diligent attender of our Meetings for Worship, as well as of those for transacting the affairs of the Church. His remarks in Monthly and Quarterly Meetings, as well as in those for Ministers and Elders, were often pertinent and valuable. He was not however in the habit of *urging* his opinions. When these were seen to differ from the prevailing sentiment of a meeting, he would, with equal modesty and cheerfulness, submit his own judgment to that of his friends. As an Elder, he cherished a feeling of affectionate sympathy with Friends engaged in the ministry of the Gospel;—sometimes imparting advice or encouragement, and occasionally accompanying them when travelling from home on religious service.

Until the last year or two of his life, our dear friend's general health had been for many years remarkably good. But whilst attending the Yearly Meeting in London in 1868, he was suddenly affected with serious illness, which obliged him to return home, and confined him to the house, and to his bed for many weeks. This illness was attended with much bodily discomfort and even suffering, which he was enabled to bear with exemplary patience and even cheerfulness. During the autumn of that year, he gradually recovered, so far as to be able to attend our usual Meetings for worship, and to enjoy social intercourse with his friends; but he was not able to return to the more public engagements of various kinds, to which much of his attention had been previously devoted.

His friends regard it as a providential arrangement, graciously designed to promote his comfort and well-being, that he was thus withdrawn, during the concluding stage of his earthly pilgrimage, from many of his former activities, and permitted to spend the late evening of life very much in the seclusion of his own home. He thus enjoyed more opportunity for retirement and meditation: and though he did not converse much on subjects of this nature, yet from hints that occasionally dropped from him, there is reason to believe he was much engaged in contemplating the nearness of eternity; whilst the serene expression of his countenance, and his quiet habitual cheerfulness, might well be regarded as an index to the peaceful state of his mind. His last illness was short, and after a few days of only partial consciousness, he was permitted gently to pass away, having recently entered on his 79th year.

SARAH THOMPSON,   50 29 10 mo. 1869

   Kendal. A Minister. Wife of James Thompson.

Believers in all ages have borne testimony to the benefit which they have derived from Christian biography, when faithfully written. The experiences of those who have trodden the path before us, the difficulties, dangers, and trials which they have encountered, and the way in which they have been enabled to overcome, are often animating and helpful to those who are still travelling onwards in the same path. In this light a short account of this beloved Friend may not be without instruction to others.

Sarah Thompson was the daughter of Isaac and Sarah Bass of Brighton, where she was born in 1819. Her life afforded ample proof of the blessed effects of parental care and training. Some early memoranda in her own handwriting from nine to twelve years of age, while testifying to her sense of the evil of her heart, evince her earnest desire to belong to the fold of the Saviour, and to cherish a thankful spirit for the blessings of which she was a partaker.

"Brighton, 21st of Twelfth month, 1828. Today in the first meeting my dear cousin Daniel Pryor Hack kneeled down and appeared in supplication for some time. I fear I have not such trust in the Lord as I ought to. I think I do not thank that great and good Being enough, for all the comforts His gracious hand bestows on me; but I hope that as I grow older, I shall thank Him better."

"22nd of Twelfth month, 1828. I hope I am getting more strength in the Lord; and hope I shall not forget that His ways are ways of pleasantness, and all His paths are peace."

"16th of Fifth month, 1831. Yesterday in the morning meeting I got a little more still than I do commonly. I am so very naughty, I fear; but I hope the Lord of all mercies will, by His chastening hand, bring me to His fold, from whence if I never strayed, I should be happy within, if trials oppress me without."

Being an only daughter, she enjoyed, as she advanced in life, the close companionship of her mother, to whose consistent example and wise counsel she frequently referred in later years. Like her mother, she was in the practice of early rising, that she might devote a quiet season of retirement, before the family assembled at the breakfast table, to the devout reading of the Holy Scriptures, and to meditation and prayer;—a practice which, no doubt, tended largely to the formation of the Christian character of both. By a friend who knew her intimately, she was characterized as " abounding in prayer." She enjoyed a lively sense of the immediate presence of her Lord, in which she could approach Him in child-like simplicity and faith. Having first sought to give her heart to the Lord, she experienced the joy and peace of such a dedication. Life was felt to have higher aims and purposes than had before been known; and her every day duties were performed with cheerfulness and alacrity.

After leaving school, she became associated with her mother in a great variety of philan-thropic and charitable agencies; and to the end of life she delighted to minister to the wants of the ignorant and the destitute, by whom her visits were warmly welcomed. Being deprived of her mother in 1852, and continuing to live with her father during the two or three remain-ing years of his life, she sought with great filial devotedness to contribute to his comfort and happiness, and to soothe his declining years.

While devoting the prime of her time and strength to the calls of religious and social

N

duties, she did not neglect the cultivation of her intellectual powers, and the storing of her mind with useful knowledge. For this purpose she long kept up the practice of systematic reading, and frequently made summaries of the contents of the books which she perused, with occasional comments or criticisms of her own. She possessed a cultivated taste for poetry, as is evidenced by a considerable collection of original poems which she has left behind, together with a number of translations from the German hymn-writers. The following stanzas referring to the loss of her mother, form the concluding stanzas of a piece which she wrote on the words of our Lord in John xv., 7, "Abide in Me :"

"And since Thou hast been pleased to call
   A tender parent to her rest,
Upon me let her mantle fall,
   And bind it closely round my breast.

And on my spirit richly pour
   A double portion from above
Of all the excellence she bore,
   Her zeal, her fervour, and her love.

So shall the blessings which she sought
   With earnest prayer, with sighs and tears,
For me, whilst yet I knew Thee not
   In childhood's young and thoughtless years,—

Be granted now with power divine
   To make me what I ought to be ;
Whilst here, a pilgrim wholly Thine,—
   Then live eternally with Thee.—*Amen.*"

In the summer of 1858 she was married to James Thompson of Kendal, where the remainder of her life was spent in the enjoyment of a bright and happy union. On the 6th of Sixth month she makes the following record in her journal: " I have now entered upon the last week of my single life ; and the important step to be taken next Fifth day still looks bright in prospect, as it has long done. A new and changed state and position await me, and I must seek earnestly for grace to act in accordance with my ever blessed Heavenly Father's will. My own concerns have of late so much occupied my time and thoughts, that I feel a jealousy in my heart, lest I be too much taken up with my new and happy state, and not make sufficient effort of self-denial and watchfulness unto prayer. O Lord, be very near unto me, and strengthen me to perform all the important duties of a wife, with affection, submission, and a constant regard to Thy glory; that we may be one in our efforts to devote ourselves wholly to Thy service, and not permit self-indulgence to benumb the energies of our souls."

About three years previous to this important event, she had felt it required of her to speak in our meetings for worship. On the evening of her father's interment, when a large company was gathered in the house, she, for the first time, engaged publicly in prayer and thanksgiving: and a few months afterwards, when on a visit to some relatives at Chelmsford, she spoke in a meeting for worship with much sweetness on the words, "Honour the Lord with thy substance, and with the first fruits of all thine increase." Thus another sphere of service for her Lord opened before her, claiming the warm dedication of her heart, and a watchful care to know and follow the pointings of her Guide. Her feelings in connection with the ministry of the Gospel are thus given, in a letter which she addressed to a near relative: "14th of Second month, 1856. Truly the work to which I have at times believed myself called, is one of a nature very crucifying to the flesh, and to the pride and reason of the natural part in us. It is wonderful that such a poor, weak, ignorant person as I am should thus be called upon, and I am at times almost ready to question the possibility of its rectitude; and yet when the duty does present, there is such a constraining power accompanying, that I dare not resist; and we know that 'God chooses the weak and base things to confound the mighty; and even things that are not, to bring to nought things that are, that no flesh should glory in His presence.' I have been most mercifully dealt with, and though I may not have experienced very powerful manifestations of Divine influence on having yielded to impressions of duty, yet I think I may say, and with humility be it spoken, a calm serenity has pervaded my mind, which has often lasted for a considerable time; and holy truths have opened with a clearness and freshness to my understanding but seldom known before; whilst a deeper relish for heavenly things, by no means lessening my enjoyment of life, has been experienced. I hope in thus expressing a little of what I have felt, I am not exceeding the bounds of propriety; for I know these are points on which great care should be exercised not to say too much; but thou hast manifested so much kind interest towards me, that I longed to tell thee somewhat how it is with me, and hope thou wilt encourage or repress my expressions of this kind as thou mayest feel right."

In the year 1865 she accompanied Rebecca Collins of New York in a religious visit to Friends in Germany and the South of France,

for which she was somewhat specially qualified;
not only by her ability to sympathize with the
exercises of her dear companion, and to take
part with her in meetings for worship, but also
by her knowledge of the German and French
languages, and by the lengthened visits which
she had previously paid to some intimate friends
in the South of France, and at Minden.

Her cheerful and lively disposition endeared
her to her younger friends; and her loving interest
in them, especially those nearly related to her,
was shown in the frequent letters of encouragement and counsel which she addressed to them,
entering into their difficulties and discourage-
ments, sharing their joys, or pointing out to them
where danger or temptation might lie.   She
always enjoyed their company, and while heartily
entering into their pursuits and amusements,
often sought, in an interesting and unobtrusive
way, to direct the conversation to more serious
and important subjects.

She was much beloved by the Friends of the
Quarterly Meeting to which she belonged.   On
two or three occasions she received "Minutes"
from her Monthly Meeting to visit the meetings,
and in some places the families of Friends, com-
posing it; and when about a year before her

death she was attacked by a malignant complaint, which might have been regarded by many as a warrant for relaxing their religious service, she continued her visits in a neighbouring Monthly Meeting, to within a few days of submitting to a serious surgical operation.

The means taken to arrest the progress of the disease proved unavailing; but she was preserved throughout in a calm trust in the goodness of her Father in heaven, and in a loving submission to His will. On the morning of the operation she wrote in her journal: " 21st of Twelfth month, 1868. Near the end of the year, and the end of my book.—Is it also near the end of my life? This is an eventful episode in my life. To-day I am to undergo an operation for the removal of a small cancerous tumour. * * * I rose earlier than usual, and had a precious time alone. Prayer arose in my heart for myself and all connected. After breakfast, kneeling almost in the same place, my dearest poured forth a prayer so similar, that I felt we are united in the closest of bonds; and faith was granted that help would not fail in the needful time. * * Though we have sought the advice of the best human skill we are aware of, I feel that the future is in His hands alone, who is the ever wise and good

Arbiter of life. Lord! into Thy care and keeping once more do I commit myself, and all near and dear to me, for time and for eternity. *Amen*."

A week later she writes to some near relatives : "A week ago to-day my hand was forbidden for a time all active employment, and I am desirous that this first effort should be used, to acknowledge with grateful love your kindness and sympathy for me and my dearest James during our recent trying experience ; and to raise a tribute of thanksgiving and praise to a gracious Lord, who, as we have been enabled to trust in Him, has been faithful to His own promise, ' I will never leave thee, nor forsake thee.' I can truly say I have felt undeserving of so much kindness and tender consideration from relatives and friends. * * * The supporting and guiding hand of my gracious Lord has been sweetly extended, far beyond what I could have anticipated ; and precious as the xxiii. Psalm has often felt to me, I never before so much *experienced* its fulness from beginning to end. * * * * I cannot do better than close [my letter] with the words of the Psalmist, ' Oh ! magnify the Lord with me, and let us exalt His name together.'"

"Third month 19th, 1869. Gratitude for abounding mercies is often the covering of my spirit; and I am able to leave the result of the effort now being made [for my recovery] in His hands, who orders all things well for those who trust in Him."

" 8th of Sixth month, 1869. • • • • I still have to walk by faith, not by sight; and to learn this lesson more fully (I am ready to think) has been one important need for passing through the present dispensation. Very precious is it to feel that I am under the care and guidance of an all-wise - and all-merciful Lord, who knows exactly the treatment I am most in need of, to make me what I ought to be; and in His holy care I desire to leave myself, whether my return to my dear husband and home be sooner or later."

A second operation being considered needful, she writes to her sister-in-law about a week previous : " Having sought to adopt the right course, we must afresh resign the case into His hands who only knows what is right and best for us, and can bless the means used for cure, if consistent with His holy will. I am favoured thus to leave it, not feeling *anxious* about the future,—a mercy which I feel assured comes directly from Him who promises, ' as thy day, so shall thy strength be ;' for of myself I could not be thus calm."

Thus committing herself with unswerving faith into the hands of her gracious Lord, whose faithfulness she had often proved, she sweetly and cheerfully resigned herself, when the appointed time came, to the last and only resource of her medical advisers. The shock proved too great for the system, into which the disease had made deep inroads, and in less than forty-eight hours she sank under it. Being informed when in a very exhausted state that there was no hope of her recovery, and that the end must be near, she faintly replied, " Is it so ?—Blessed Jesus ;" and shortly passed away.

ESTHER THOMPSON,   69   7 11 mo. 1869
    Hesketh Newmarket.   Widow of Henry Thompson.

RICHARD WILLIAM THOMPSON,
    Southport.   24 15   1 mo. 1870
Son of Josiah and Margaret Thompson.

This young Friend was laid low in the very dawn of manhood, by a fatal illness of twelve months' continuance : in the course of which he attained, through some struggles and conflicts of spirit, to that peace of mind which the Lord Jesus bequeathed to those who give up their hearts to Him. And as he fervently *longed* that all his young acquaintances might have their hearts also turned to the Lord, and expressed how he should rejoice if anything he could say or do, might influence them to that end, it is hoped by a review of his life and last days, this wish may be in degree realized. " He mourns the dead, who lives as they desire."

Richard William was the son of Josiah and Margaret Thompson, and was born at Rawden near Leeds on the 13th of Eleventh month, 1845, but his parents shortly after removed to Birkenhead. At the age of ten, their son was sent to school at Kendal, where he remained six years; and then it was decided, that he should avail himself of an opening to learn the woollen manufacturing business, with a firm in that town. This arrangement was very satisfactory to him, as he entertained a high esteem for the principals of the establishment, and preferred to remain in the country, which he had learned to love. He early gained the confidence of his employers, by his prompt and energetic business capabilities. But in consequence of the decease of a cousin who was engaged in business with his father in Liverpool, he believed it to be a duty to return home, and render what assistance he could to his beloved parent. In 1863 he entered on this new sphere with earnestness, and found his responsi-

bilities much increased, when on several occasions
he was left in charge, during his father's unavoid-
able absence from home. Before he was nineteen,
he was also entrusted with special business to
some of their connexions in the United States.

Though never very robust, he engaged in
these duties with energy and industry : but he
had also imbibed no small love for the beauties of
nature, and was fond of sketching. The periods
of relaxation from business which health seemed
to require, were therefore often spent among lakes
and mountains. He much enjoyed joining two
of his friends in a pedestrian tour of three weeks
in Norway : at other times he explored scenes
nearer home ; and in the autumn of 1868, he
accompanied an intimate friend in a visit to
France and Switzerland. In these excursions he
took many sketches, and wrote with enthusiasm
of mountains, fiords, and waterfalls. But while
absorbed with wonder and admiration, he was
accustomed, with a reflective mind, "to look
from nature up to Nature's God."

"Such scenery," he would observe, "makes
one feel the power of the great Creator." When
visiting the Falls of Niagara, he says in his
journal : "How this wondrous creation must
have struck the lonely Indian's poetic mind,—

(long before the eye of the aggressive white man
ever saw its glories,)—and impressed him with
the omnipotence of the great good Spirit!" At
the Falls of Montmorency, he had a narrow
escape from drowning by falling into one of the
rapids, and it is believed this deliverance was
ever after regarded by him as a signal mercy.

In crossing the Atlantic, we find in his
memoranda sentiments of confiding trust in the
Divine goodness, a desire for religious improvement, and gratitude for *His* protecting care who
ruleth the winds and the sea." When com-
mencing the homeward voyage he wrote : " Here
I am, nearly out of sight of land once more. I
trust my Heavenly Father, who has protected
me thus far, will bring me to my own dear home
and all I love there, in health and safety : and
that I may find myself cleaving harder to Him
every day of my life."

He took much interest in the First-day
Schools, and especially enjoyed attending the
Conference of Teachers held at Birmingham.
He was also punctual in attending meetings
for worship. He was fond of sitting up late
at night ; but from a sense of duty as to the
right way of closing the day, began to retire to
his own room exactly at ten o'clock, and it is

o

known, that when there he spent a portion of time in reading the Bible, and in prayer. His parents have the consoling belief, that their dear son was being gradually prepared for the solemn change that awaited him, though so little foreseen by them. They often remarked on his simple, child-like love and obedience ; and that the hasty and rather overbearing manner that sometimes showed itself, was being softened as he advanced in years and knowledge.

He greatly enjoyed social evenings with his friends, entering freely into their amusements ; yet he often expressed a wish that something of a less trivial character could be adopted, that would give equal enjoyment to mixed companies, and leave no sense of wasted time afterwards.

As the winter of 1868 and 69 advanced, his health was becoming more precarious, than he himself was aware of; and on the 30th of First month in the evening, as he was sitting with his parents, and copying a sketch he had taken in Rouen, a sudden fit of coughing brought on *hemorrhage from the lungs.* Nor was this a solitary attack, others followed, though he was kept very quiet, and forbidden speaking ;—till a fourth hemorrhage quite prostrated him, and for seven weeks the cough and throat being very irritable, his strength was reduced to a very low ebb. It was indeed the beginning of the end. In the Fourth month with much difficulty he was removed to Bournemouth in the South of Hampshire, being detained at Reading nearly two weeks by increased illness. On the 3rd of Fifth month, on which day also he had a slight hemorrhage, a telegram arrived, announcing the death of his cousin Arthur Henry Wilson. This, combined with his own state, produced a solemn sadness; and an increased watchfulness was observed, and earnestness for the salvation of his soul. His favourite employment of drawing was often laid aside for the reading of the Bible, especially the Psalms and New Testament; and at times he expressed a fear that *he* was too vile to *expect* to be saved.* He read very much in a little book a friend had given him, entitled "*Able to Save*," from which he derived much comfort. After deep searchings and tossings of mind, he

* The reader should not, from this expression, and from Richard William's repeated allusion to his being like the prodigal son received back again by his forgiving Father, conclude that he had followed a loose and worldly life while in health. His words are rather to be viewed as arising from that true conviction of sin, by which the Holy Spirit leads every true believer to the foot of the Cross, for pardon and reconciliation and healing.

was favoured to find peace, in the conviction
that his sins were pardoned through the blood
of Jesus. Many texts were afterwards found
marked in his Testament, which show plainly on
what his hopes were grounded, as in the iii., v.
and viii chapters of Romans, and several in other
parts, especially in John.

The disease not abating, but returning again
and again after temporary improvement, it was
concluded to return home. Malvern was tried, but
was more oppressive, and the patient was confined
to his bed. One evening he prayed, in weak but
solemn tones, for help and strength, and for
greater dedication to Him who has done so much
for us, and who gave His only Son, that through
His blood we might be saved. He ardently longed
for a clearer evidence of the presence of his
Saviour. On the 22nd of the Seventh month,
he again reached Birkenhead. To the surprise
of all, he now began to rally, and after some
weeks could sit up a little : no hemorrhage
recurred, and he was even able to be drawn in
his chair to the next room, which commanded
his favourite prospect : and here he finished some
of his Swiss sketches, sitting up two or three
hours daily. He loved to watch the sunsets, and
quoted with feeling the lines of A. A. Procter :—

"I thank Thee, O my God, who made
　　This earth so bright;
So full of splendour and of joy,
　　Beauty and light;
So many glorious things are here,
　　Noble and right."

We have not space for the whole of this hymn,
but one or two stanzas are so suited to his case,
we may rightly introduce them :

"I thank Thee more, that all our joy
　　Is touched with pain,—
That shadows fall on brightest hours,—
　　That thorns remain :—
So that earth's bliss may be our guide,
　　And not our chain.

　　*　　*　　*　　*　　*

I thank Thee, Lord, that here our souls,
　　Though amply blest,
Can never find, although they seek,
　　A perfect rest ;—
Nor ever shall, until they lean
　　On Jesus' breast ! "

As autumn advanced, a removal to Southport
was recommended; and notwithstanding the
feeble state of the invalid, it was accomplished.
In crossing the Mersey, the carriage was run on
board the steamer, and he greatly enjoyed seeing
once again the river glowing in the sunshine, with

an unusual number of boats, ships and steamers
plying about, presenting the animated scene he
had always delighted in. When about the middle,
he said, pressing his mother's hand, "This is very
nice, dearest mamma; I do enjoy this." Thus for
the last time did he cross that frequently crossed
river. In his room at Southport, he was still
able to be up a couple of hours daily; and not
willing to be idle, he had his drawing materials
out, and finished his sketch of the market-place
at Rouen. But only a few times could he resume
his favourite employment. At last he finally laid
down his pencils, and said: "There, mamma,
that is all I can do at it: I wish I could do
something for the glory of God!"

Henceforth this was his chief earthly aim.
He loved to listen to reading: but he liked to
read the Scriptures himself. It was his oft
repeated prayer, that he might become all his
Heavenly Father wished, and that he might bear
patiently all that he thought fit to send. At times
he still had fears that he was too unworthy, to
be forgiven: saying that he had never done
anything for the glory of God,—his life had
been spent unprofitably:—how could *he* find
acceptance? Yet when asked if he did not
believe in the all-sufficiency of Christ's blood,

to atone for even the worst of sinners? he exclaimed, "yes, I do believe that Christ died for sinners, most fully :—and yet is it not possible that some may be castaways? Did not even Paul fear that he might become a castaway?" He would ask how he could become regenerated, when he was so prone to sin? for the fruits of the spirit are "love, joy, peace, long-suffering, gentleness, goodness, faith, meekness, temperance :—and did he exhibit any of these? Such were his heart searchings, a part of the work of that same Holy Spirit, by which alone the fruits of true holiness can be brought forth. His favourite hymn was, "*We would see Jesus,*" which he often loved to hear read to him. Meanwhile his patience was remarkable, though in health he exhibited at times some haste of temper, when things were not exactly to his mind : but now there was an evident striving to guard against impatient thoughts or words.

On the 29th of Tenth month, he gladdened the hearts of his dear parents by telling them how peaceful he felt, and that at last he quite believed " that he should be admitted within the pearl gates,—and there, utterly unworthy though he was, appear before the great white throne, with garments washed white in the blood of the

Lamb." Then he fervently prayed that they might all meet in heaven.

A fortnight later, under extreme suffering, he exclaimed, " Mother dear ! I do not know how to bear this pain any longer. Oh pray for me ! dear mother,—that I may have patience to bear all my Heavenly Father sees fit to send : and let me never forget what my Saviour suffered for me." Fomentations were applied, and after a time an abscess discharged itself, to his great relief, but increased weakness. It was about this time, that he asked the nurse "if it was *really impossible* for him to recover ?" and on her informing him that in all human probability he could not, he was sensibly affected, and asked further, how long she thought he might linger ? He was told it was probable only a very few weeks, or it might only be *days*. Though he made no immediate reply, he was much moved at this intelligence, and afterwards said to his mother : "I did not know my end was so very near. I have had a hope that I might get better. I have enjoyed life *very* much ; but I felt if I got better, it would have to be a very different one. I should have had to devote it to the service of God :—and I have dreaded sometimes the thought of entering the world again, for fear of not being steadfast, and being led away from my duty. But if my Heavenly Father sees fit to take me *now*, I trust He will have mercy on me for Jesus' sake;—and I believe He *will* have mercy, poor prodigal that I am." He was often observed looking at the scroll-texts that were hung up near his bed, and when they were about to be changed, frequently wished them to remain. One page was headed, " The sufferings of Christ," on which he said, " I like to try to realize what Jesus suffered for me." For some time his nights were much disturbed, and he was glad when daybreak came, and he heard the tramp of men going to their early work: but as he remembered how he had been accustomed to walk in health and strength as vigorous as they, he sometimes felt distressed, yet would greet his mother with a smile, saying, " the Lord's mercies are new every morning: we must not forget to be very thankful."

As the Eleventh month wore away, he was affectionately concerned for his dear brother and sister, urging on them to be watchful and earnest in prayer, and diligent in reading the Scriptures every day: and if they had not time for a chapter or two, he advised them to commit a few verses to memory, telling them what a comfort it would be when they were laid on a sick bed, and not able to read. Speaking of the uncertainty of life, he said he had prayed for them, that they might *prepare now whilst in health* for the great change: for on a sick bed the mind is often distracted by bodily pains and weariness, and is little able either to pray or think. He spoke to them of his own case, how he regretted not having followed Christ more earnestly *whilst in health*:—and that now he trusted in His great mercy and love, in having given himself up for sinners such as he. He hoped to welcome them in the heavenly land; though if he entered there, it would not be for anything he had ever done, but through the precious blood of the Saviour. His affectionate feelings were also drawn out for his sorrowing mother, who told him how she dreaded their separation:—" well," he said, " we must not look ahead, but live one day at a time, receiving the mercies of each day thankfully."

He thought much of the spiritual condition of his young friends and acquaintances, including the young men in his father's office, for whom he desired that with their praiseworthy diligence and care, they might not follow business too eagerly; for, said he, " they must not neglect their soul's salvation." Like messages did he send to others, in a very fervent manner declaring how he longed they might all be led to repentance, and how he should rejoice if *anything he could say or do* might influence them. On one of these occasions he asked his mother if he had said too much? " I am afraid of saying too much." he observed : " but *I do long* that they should *all* come to Christ :—for where should I be now, if it were not for Him ? "

As the time of Christmas approached, he was desirous as usual to make little presents ; and, unknown to the recipients, had by the aid of others prepared various last mementoes of his love :—remembering also the domestics to whom he felt particularly grateful, and whom he often addressed with singularly appropriate texts of Scripture. Though a solemn and affecting time, it was a day of quiet and uninterrupted happiness, of that character that blended earthly with heavenly enjoyment ;—the unbroken family never to meet again. One of their near connexions, of those who were a year before enjoying health and happiness below, removed to the higher happiness in heaven,—another following,—many widely separated from them,—and yet in the sense of mutual love, and gratitude for many mercies, it was a day of chastened joy !

On the New Year's Day of 1870, in view of

the inevitable progress of the disease, Richard William closed his eyes in prayer, and said, " O blessed Lord ! be pleased to comfort my dearest mother with Thy Holy Spirit. Bless and protect her : and show her that her treasure is in heaven, incorruptible, and that fadeth not away. And if it please Thee, forsake *me* not in my hour of need ; but in Thy great mercy accept me for Jesus' sake. Enable me to lay *firm* hold on Him as the Rock immovable, and forgive my many and great sins." The rest of the prayer was inaudible.

On the night of the 12th he suffered much for several hours, and in the morning the doctor expressed his opinion that he could not continue. He was favoured however with great calmness and peace, repeating his admonitions to his brother and sisters " to look to Jesus, and *make sure* of Him in time of health, and not to leave repentance to a sick bed, which was not the best place for this needful work." Waking early on the 13th he was full of gratitude for a comfortable sleep of two hours. Again he thought of his companions in business, sending his love to them, with his desire that they would not let business cares engross too much of their attention, but that they would " seek *first* the kingdom of heaven." He also spoke of the care of his Heavenly Father in providing so many comforts,—a kind doctor, and invaluable nurse. He feared he had been very selfish through all his illness, and had borne his pains more like a child than in a manly, Christian spirit. But he had a still higher theme for gratitude. After some sleep, he exclaimed distinctly:—" O mother! it is wonderful!—wonderful!—that He should receive the poor prodigal; for

> ' Nothing in my hand I bring,
> Simply to Thy cross I cling:
> Naked, come to Thee for dress;
> Helpless, look to Thee for grace:
> Vile, I to the Fountain fly:—
> Wash me, Saviour, or I die.

> ' While I draw this fleeting breath,
> When my eyelids close in death,
> When I soar to worlds unknown,
> See Thee on Thy judgment-throne,—
> Rock of ages, cleft for me,
> Let me hide myself in Thee!"

These stanzas he repeated correctly, and then went on to say, "and yet He has washed me clean in His blood, and will give me the victory:— and I can and do rejoice, and could sing aloud His praise:—but that is for the joys hereafter,

P

when I have entered the pearl gates! But perhaps I am saying too much: and yet I must not let in the tempter now; for, through unbounded unmerited grace, he is put under. The victory is won, through Him who will keep us to the end: 'for no man shall pluck them out of my Father's hand!'" After thinking if he had any outward matters to settle, he returned to the great theme: saying, " all is so calm and sweet, it must proceed from God."

The 14th of First month arrived, and waking he said: "Dear father! I think my feet are on the Rock:—my heart feels easy. 'He chasteneth every son whom He receiveth.'" At another time, "I feel like the prodigal son, whom the Father stretched out his arms to receive." Again, "Give my messages to my fellow-workers at the office; * * * Tell ——, not to trust too much to works, though we must seek to work for God's glory; but our *trust* must be in Christ. * * Dear H. I wish I had talked more to him when I was able." On the suggestion being made, that the few words he had been enabled to say of late, might be just as valuable as more said at a previous time, he replied, "Ah yes! it is not always in the multitude of words!"

As night approached, he was absorbed in

prayer;—solemnly and fervently he said, " Now that we are all assembled together, in deep humility before Thee, enable us to put up our feeble petitions. We thank Thee for Thy many mercies, and for dealing so gently with us. And now that we are about to separate, it may be in a longer or a shorter time, may we all be permitted to meet around Thy throne. O Thou omnipotent and omnipresent God! bless all who are laid on a bed of sickness, and who are longing for rest. Enable all to *seek first* the kingdom of heaven and its righteousness, and all things needful shall be added. Bless the kind creature who has ministered so faithfully, many days and nights, to my wants through this sickness :—but I know Thou wilt bless her!"

At midnight, in feeble accents, he prayed again :—"Almighty God! we dare but approach Thee with fear and trembling, for our garments are defiled ;—and Thou wilt find the talents Thou hast given me rather depreciated than increased : but Christ has been before;—and, clothed in the righteousness of Christ, we are accepted, and can appear without fear—without fear—accepted, most merciful Father, in Jesus! Amen! Amen!"

About half-past four on the morning of the 15th, his last audible supplication was breathed :

" O Lord Jesus ! through Thy blood-shedding I
trust Thou hast admitted me into the guest-
chamber, with Thy other guests and disciples.
So let it be, O Lord !"—and soon after added,
" O Lord, enable us to do Thy will." He became
restless, but could scarcely make known his
wants. He looked earnestly to the scroll of texts,
and within an hour of his last breath, he read
aloud part of the 3rd and 4th verses of the
iii. chapter of Colossians : " For ye are dead, and
your life is hid with Christ in God. When
Christ, who is our life, shall appear,—then shall
ye also appear with Him in glory." His dear
aunt finished the passage as his voice failed, and
proceeded with the next sentence on the scroll,
" for to me to live is Christ," which he promptly
finished, laying his hand on hers,—" *and to die
is gain.*" These consolations abode with him ;
after a time he said again to his dear father sitting
by him, " *Christ our life :*"—and these were his last
words, excepting " *quick*," or " *quickly*," the
meaning of which was not understood.

His breathing now became shorter, and it
was evident that the long-looked-for end was at
hand ; when those of the family who were not
already present were summoned, and were only
just in time to witness the last quiet breathings

of the sweet spirit that was entering the pearl gates, to be presented, as they reverently believed, "before the great white Throne, in robes washed and made white in the blood of the Lamb."

Edwin Thompson, M.B.C.M., M.R.C.S., *Birkenhead*.   22 21   3 mo. 1870 Died at Edinburgh.   Son of the late George Thompson, of Rock Ferry.

In preparing a brief record of the earthly life of one, whose humility and diffidence of his own attainments were so remarkable as in the present instance, it is difficult even to give the statements of those, who had no relationship with him to render them partial, without appearing to indulge in something of that adulation, from which his own meek and gentle spirit would have shrunk:—but the conviction that he was what he was by the grace of God, and the hope that his example may be an incitement to the young, and particularly to those about to enter upon the *medical* profession, and to encounter the snares and temptations which beset the youthful student's path, is the inducement for presenting this account of his short life.

Edwin Thompson was the youngest son of George and Eliza Thompson, and was born at Liverpool on the 18th of Sixth month, 1847.

From his earliest infancy, he was of a particularly sensitive nature, manifesting great tenderness of spirit, and much susceptibility to religious impressions; his tears often silently flowing, when anything was read which touched his deepest feelings. When about six years of age he had a very serious illness, which greatly prostrated his strength, and left but slender hopes of his recovery. He was placed for a short time with a kind Friend, well known to the family, at the sea-side, none of his home circle being able then to accompany him; but he pined so much for the society of those he loved most, that as soon as it could be arranged, his mother, with the brother who had always been his dearest associate, went with him to Southport, where he regained his former health and buoyancy of spirits. His restoration was felt to be peculiarly an answer to prayer, granted on submission to an apprehended Divine requiring. He was then earnestly dedicated to Him, who had thus again bestowed the precious loan : and graciously was this dedication owned. For he was a child taught of God; and never during his short and lovely career, did he cause any uneasiness to those who loved him most; except from the conviction that he was so maturing for heaven, that they might have to mourn an early separation.

His medical attendant advised his being sent to a school in the south, for the more complete re-establishment of his health; accordingly he went for two or three years to Sidcot School, where he acquired complete health and vigour. Upon leaving Sidcot, he was placed under the care of Charles Willmore at Alderley. There he gained the love of his teachers and companions, and formed friendships which ripened as he advanced in years. Charles Willmore writes of him: " He gave a healthy earnest tone to all he associated with, and was a real merry boy none the less. * * * Whatever he did, he did it heartily, as to the Lord, and not unto man." When Charles Willmore removed to Queenwood, Edwin continued his studies at Owen's College, Manchester; the parents of one of his schoolfellows, who was about to attend the same college, most kindly offering him a home at their house while thus engaged. The mother of the family (for every member of which he always entertained the most grateful affection,) thus writes after his decease. " How much we all loved dear Edwin! he was particularly dear to me, for I felt his influence for good in every thing, in the smallest every-day incidents of home life ; not so much in words spoken, (and they were not withheld when they could comfort or encourage those around him,) but in his loving sympathy. His power to perceive motives was singularly keen and correct ; his quick appreciation of the ridiculous was great, but I do not recollect a single instance when it ever hurt the feelings of others. His loving interest [at a later period] in my precious invalid son's state was great. I well remember, though not personally present, hearing of his kneeling in earnest prayer in a little family gathering one First-day morning, while staying with us at Ventnor ; my brother R. H. told me, ' Our meeting of an hour and a half's duration was a remarkably blessed one.' During his studies at Owen's College he would tell me of advancement in his class, or of praises received ; but somehow it savoured more of gratitude than of self-exaltation : and another thing—his purity was felt and very frequently remarked, by every one of our friends who knew much of him. But it is difficult to pourtray a life like dear Edwin's. It was such a spiritual one ; and when we call it to mind, we should have known almost it was not to be a long one."

It had been proposed to Edwin before leaving

Alderley, that if it accorded with his own taste and judgment, he should study for the Medical profession. At first he shrank from it, fearing he was not adapted for so responsible a career; but as it quietly and prayerfully rested on his mind, he believed it would be right to prepare for it. On being reminded of the snares and temptations to which the course of a medical student would expose him, he replied, he had fully considered them, but believed he should be preserved. It was also suggested to him, how much a medical man had in his power in a mental and spiritual, as well as in a physical point of view;—this also had largely occupied his thoughts, as he then expressed, and afterwards manifested. In illustration of this, we may quote the words of an invalid Friend respecting him ;—" He was so loving, so tender, so true. I shall never forget his sweet little visits to me on a First-day evening, when I was a prisoner at the Baths in Edinburgh. I have often thought and spoken of them since ; and hoped that if my life were spared, I might one day look upon his sweet face again somewhere ; and often I used to rejoice, in thinking how many a sufferer's bed-side would be cheered by his gentle presence. I remember now the feeling remark of the Scotch bath-maid after she had let him out one day : ' It would do any sick body good to see that nice young man by his bedside,' a remark in which I fully united. But God's ways are not our ways, nor His thoughts our thoughts ; He had higher and more blessed work in store for him. Ours is the loss, His the gain."

He was seventeen years of age, when he commenced his course of medical study in Edinburgh; and many have been the testimonials received of his circumspect conduct during those few years, and of his persevering efforts to do good. A kind Friend, in whose hospitable home he was ever made a welcome visitor, says, " From the very first of his residence in Edinburgh, he became a beloved member of the little meeting of Friends there. He took a lively part in all the social, and did not hold back from an earnest participation in the still higher interests of the little church. His regular attendance of Meetings for Worship, his serious manner, and his occasional vocal offerings, afforded refreshing evidence that he was truly uniting in worship. Still in very affectionate remembrance with us, are times when his voice was heard in solemn supplication ; and one day is especially remembered when many were absent, and the younger members held the usual meeting. It seemed that a fresh outpouring of the Holy Spirit had visited them. Edwin's voice was first heard. He quoted the text, 'My people have committed two evils; they have forsaken Me, the Fountain of living waters, and have hewn out to themselves cisterns, broken cisterns, that can hold no water:' and a sense is still felt of the solemnity and power with which he continued to speak on this subject, directing to the Fountain of living water. 'They drank of that spiritual Rock which followed them, and that Rock was Christ.'"

Another of his dear Edinburgh friends says, " I remember so well one First-day evening when we were sitting round the fire in the twilight, mamma had been speaking to Edwin, I think about the ' young men who are strong and have overcome the wicked one,' and I saw Edwin smile, and heard him say softly, half to himself, 'Ah, but I'm only one of the *little children* still,' And so indeed he was, and *is*, and I have been thinking we must not be wanting him back again; for surely ' of such as he is the kingdom of heaven.' I shall never forget the heavenly feeling that came over our meeting, the first time he prayed vocally; and the look of joy and peace on his face when we spoke to him afterwards."

In conjunction with one or two other student friends, Edwin commenced a small Sabbath School in one of the lowest parts of the town. He was very diligent in his attendance when his duties permitted, and the school has been successfully carried on since. One of his associates in the work says, " We miss dear Edwin's bright and happy face continually, especially on First-days, and at our Student's Bible Meeting."

An intimate friend of the family, expressing his deep sympathy with them in their bereavement, wrote : " During late visits to Edinburgh, Edwin and I had much pleasant converse together, and I had learnt to know and appreciate the *deeper* side of his character. Above all, it was a good thing to find a young physician, who had not lost one shade of his natural tenderness for the suffering of others, by reason of being brought into daily contact with it. • • The dead often take a great place in life, and do more to keep the living straight, and pure, and high in their aims, than living companions. In such a bereavement as yours, one may be resigned to the will of God, in simple faith that what He does is best ; but still the mind is bewildered, and wonders why it is, that in a world where good and true men, who would fight all their lives on the right side, can so ill be spared, we should so often see such suddenly taken away? Most heartily do I sympathize with what you say about work to be done elsewhere."*

The following is an extract of a letter addressed to one of Edwin's intimate friends: " Your kind note has just arrived, bearing the sorrowful tidings of the departure of our dear friend and brother Edwin Thompson. I can scarcely believe that that lovely fellow, so full of fun, can now be lying still and motionless. It is a heavy loss to you, and perhaps no one will miss him more than you; but let us strive to feel more that it is the will of God; for we have great reason to believe that he was living for a higher and better life. There was one little incident which has given me great pleasure in remembering. I once heard him offer up a prayer in the Meeting; and this gave me more real insight into his inner life, than all my previous knowledge of him. I say it is the will of our Heavenly Father, therefore let us bear it with joy; and

* Soon after these words were penned, the writer himself was called suddenly from the midst of a career, in which his high talents and earnest devotion to the right and the true, gave promise of increasingly extensive usefulness, to that higher service of which he often loved to think and speak.

Q

though I write this with tears, I can rejoice to think that he was a child of God, and therefore it was the will of God that he should depart. It seems strange that such should be called at so early an age; just at the time to be useful to others, but I thoroughly believe he has a work to do that we know little of."

One of his fellow-students thus writes: "It is his *goodness* that I chiefly remember now; I have heard many talk of it. There seems to be no better word for summing up his character than this, he was very good; and that is a grand character at twenty-two. I remember one occasion when we (the members of the *Medical Students' Christian Association*) were having a supper party. When Edwin's turn came to speak, I shall never forget how there, and in those circumstances, when many men would hide their religion, he earnestly and yet so modestly spoke of the reality of eternal things; and hoped the young men his companions would think of these things. It has pleased God to call him early to the great reward; graciously freeing him from the burden and heat of the day. For us it is left to continue the fight; but now with one tie less to bind us to this life, and one link more to join us to the next." Another young student, present at the supper just alluded to, says : " Edwin spoke impressively, and the more so, that up to that time the proceedings had been more entertaining than solemn. His serious tone and words gave at once a different character to the gathering; and many remember the effect they produced."

A lady resident in Edinburgh, in acknowledging a photograph, continues : "Truly precious will dear Edwin's memory ever be to all his friends here ; truly may it be said, that to know him was to love him. His bright and genial spirit, his genuine kind-heartedness, and his intellectual attainments, rendered him a delightful companion to old and young, and he was always a welcome visitor." Another lady, whose son was a fellow-student with Edwin, writes : " Never did I hear the name of Edwin Thompson, but it was coupled with admiration and respect. ' Pure as gold, and true as steel,' are the words of my son regarding him." The son alluded to wrote as follows on hearing of his death : " It is but a few months since my father died ; and I can never forget how (during his illness) he used to come to my room in the infirmary, and cheer me with hopes that all might yet be well. When the end did come, his letter from Thirsk arrived ; so full of sympathy and loving-kindness, it was

evident that he had passed through the same
sorrow, and he made me feel that I had a
comforter. 'We must both try and help to form
the stay of our widowed mothers,' was a part of
his loving consolation."

About the middle of his course of study, a
break of several months occurred; Edwin having
been requested by a Friend to accompany his son
in delicate health, on a Continental journey, as
medical attendant and companion. This pro-
position caused him deep and anxious thought,
so much did he feel the responsibility at his age
of such an undertaking. But after prayer for
Divine guidance, he felt it right to accept the
situation; and his letters whilst absent evince
his earnest endeavours faithfully to fulfil the
trust reposed in him. In one of these letters
addressed to a friend in affliction, after speaking
of the comfort experienced in trial by the
Christian believer, he writes: "May this blessed
faith in Jesus be always yours and mine! God
grant that it may so overrule our actions, that we
may lead others, especially those near and dear
to us, to the same blessed faith." Very interesting
too were his allusions to the different places
visited. He had an ardent and enthusiastic
mind, and intensely appreciated the beauties of

natural scenery, and the historic associations of
Italy and Egypt. His enjoyment of the voyage
up the Nile was greatly enhanced by the company
of an intimate friend and his companion, who
were also travelling on account of health.

The beloved companion and fellow-student
who was more acquainted than any one else
with the details of his medical course, gives
the following particulars : " He was a diligent
student, and took great delight in his work; this
was often very marked, and these qualities of
zeal and delight exercised a good influence on
his fellow-students and others. He was almost
universally popular, and among young men of very
different characters and dispositions. He showed
a remarkable courage in one so young, in speaking
plainly and openly to a friend when he saw him
in fault, even at the risk of offending him. In
the early part of his Edinburgh life, he pursued
with great zest the study of Anatomy; and in
his third year, was requested by the Professor to
become Prosector, to prepare dissections for his
class demonstrations. His great care and exact-
ness enabled him to discover the function of a
nerve which had long puzzled Physiologists. His
notes of lectures were models of neatness ; and
were often sought after to read up by other

students, who had been less diligent in note-taking. This love of order was one of his most striking characteristics. He took a great interest in the Royal Medical Society, (of which he was Secretary for one year,) was outspoken in debate, and freely gave his time to promote its interests among the students. He was very fond of surgery, and was especially skilful in the use of the mechanical appliances connected with it. His views of medicine were liberal, and he seemed to dread the sectarianism he was likely to meet with in after life. He spoke frequently against the dogmatism of some who denounced all as quacks, who were not strictly orthodox in their therapeutics; and his own aim was, if possible, to take an independent course in his practice. He is believed to have made all his affairs (even the most trivial) subjects of prayer, and his implicit trust in a loving Almighty Father was often marked. He would frequently say with delight, "How everything has turned out for the best! I could not have wished it otherwise." One of his great characteristics was his firm adherence to principle. He held his opinions strongly sometimes, so as to appear presumptuous, and some would take offence; but his mind was always receptive of truth, and he was a careful and diligent disciple. The appointments he held show how his character and abilities were appreciated by his teachers."

One of the Professors of the University thus wrote after Edwin's death : " I knew your son Edwin, as all his teachers and fellow-students did, as one of those who was a credit to the University as a student, and gave the promise of being a credit to it as a practitioner. I was brought in contact with him, not merely as a member of my class, but as a valued attendant on my late patient and friend ———; and my estimate of your son was such, that I had destined him to be my House Physician in the Clinical Wards last winter. For reasons which I need not notice, this arrangement was not carried out. I am truly saddened, to think that a life of so much promise has been cut short."

Whilst he was in Edinburgh, a sister, seven years younger than himself, was attacked with a lingering illness. His gentle care and tender attention to her during his vacations at home, were most striking to all who witnessed them, and in speaking of her after her decease to one of his associates, he said he believed she was now a ministering spirit; and it seemed to him as if she were sometimes in close communion with his spirit, influencing to good.

In the Spring of 1869 Edwin obtained, by Examination, the Diploma of Member of the Royal College of Surgeons of England, and then proceeded to Paris, where he passed a few weeks visiting the various Medical Schools, &c. Whilst thus engaged his father was taken ill, and though after a time he was thought to be recovering, he was suddenly and unexpectedly removed by death. The shock was very awful, and Edwin was telegraphed for. His presence at home was most soothing and comforting. In that home where his strongest affections were centred, no ungentle word or look is ever remembered from him :—it is impossible to say what he was to each member of the family circle ;—he ever appeared as a sunbeam to those around him ;—it seemed as if a cloud never darkened his sky ; or if it did, his eye rested calmly on the " silver lining ;"— and he comforted others " with the comfort wherewith he himself was comforted of God."

On returning to Edinburgh, he took for a few months the position of Resident Surgeon in the Children's Hospital, where he was greatly beloved by all in the house, and particularly by the children. A Friend who visited him there

thus alludes to it: " I feel to-day that amidst the
abounding calls for thanksgiving, one is, that my
gracious Lord and Master permitted that I should
meet with dear Edwin in his work at Edinburgh
in Eighth month last. It cheered me to see him
loving and caressing the little patients, carrying
one in his arms from ward to ward of the
Children's Hospital, as he showed me through it,
and his own room, &c. There seemed a wealth
of promise for future service on earth, in his
young dedicated life ; and very fully I rejoiced
over him, little thinking that his delicate kindness, and look of tender love as the cab drove off,
were seen and felt for the last time." Very interesting were the details he sent home of his work
among the children,—" my babies," as he loved
to style them, telling how he had taught those
who were recovering to sing hymns at the bed-
sides of their companions, before settling for the
night. The matron whose kind co-operation in
his plans he much valued, said of him when
lamenting his early removal, that she believed
he lived in a state of daily preparation for a
better world. And thus with his loins girded,
and his lamp burning, he was ready for the
summons of his Lord, when it came at an
unexpected moment.

In the summer of 1869, Edwin graduated as Bachelor of Medicine, and Master of Surgery, in Edinburgh University. Shortly afterwards an important post becoming vacant for a time in the Royal Infirmary, through the illness of one of the Resident Physicians, Edwin's application for it was accepted ; and though his services were not required so long as had been at first anticipated, he considered the experience gained to have been advantageous to him. Immediately on relinquishing this situation another opening offered. A medical friend at Thirsk having occasion to leave his practice for a few months, Edwin took it during his absence. After this he returned to Edinburgh, to occupy the position of Resident Physician in the Lock Hospital and fever wards of the Royal Infirmary, where his active services were cut short by the fever which terminated his life. One of the principal Physicians thus wrote to his mother after his death : " Ever since he came to reside in the Infirmary here, in charge of the wards with which I am more immediately connected, I was greatly impressed with the gentle, kindly, amiable demeanour, and truly Christian spirit, which uniformly characterized your son ; and by which he attached to himself many friends. By all in the

house,—fellow-residents, nurses and patients,—
he was much beloved, as was evinced by the deep
concern all manifested, and very many expressed,
during his illness; and by none more than by
Drs. —— and ——. No brother could have
shown your son more devoted attention than did
they. By night and by day, when their duties
permitted, they watched anxiously by his bedside,
and did for him all that thoughtful skill could
suggest. To Dr. —— I myself feel deeply
grateful for his assiduous attention. For it was
an unspeakable comfort to be able to confide
the care of your son, to one so intensely and
anxiously interested in his recovery. I speak
thus strongly; feeling assured that it will gratify
you to learn how much your son had endeared
himself to his fellow-residents, to evoke such
brotherly devotion, not only from one, but from
all of them. Permit me, Madam, to assure you
that no one offers you deeper or truer sympathy
in this most sad bereavement, than those connected with the Infirmary, where your son
laboured so diligently, so generously, so ably,
so lovingly."

It was after attending indefatigably to his
duties at the Infirmary for about five weeks, that
he was taken ill of Typhus fever. His symptoms

were quite favourable, and he fully anticipated recovery : so that on his mother desiring to go to him, he particularly requested she would not do so ; as his anxiety for her would be great, and might be prejudicial to him, and he had most efficient nursing, and the best medical care. He was perfectly calm and composed during his illness. One of his young friends writes : "About a week after the commencement of the fever, I called in to see him early in the morning, just after he had awoke from a sound sleep. He was looking brighter than usual, and very happy and contented. Among other things I expressed the hope that his illness would terminate favourably, and that he might soon be restored to good health, (which opinion I had held from the first ;) and that God would be near to comfort and cheer him in his sickness. I quoted a few lines of Whittier's, " The healing of his seamless dress is by our beds of pain," &c. I also quoted to him the text, " He shall give His angels charge over thee to keep thee in all thy ways ;" to which he replied, ' *Very sweet to think of,—very sweet !* ' "

The accounts sent home of his progress were most encouraging for a fortnight, until the *crisis* occurred ; and as no improvement then appeared, his family were telegraphed to. They started by the first train for Edinburgh, but only arrived in time to watch him for four hours of apparent unconsciousness, and to witness his peaceful close! About an hour previously, he was much convulsed; and during this distressing conflict vocal prayer was offered, that if it were not the will of our Heavenly Father to spare his life, He would grant him a calm and peaceful dismissal, with an abundant entrance into His everlasting Kingdom; and that submission might be given under the bereavement. The words were scarcely uttered, when the convulsions ceased, and the breathing became nearly as gentle as that of a sleeping child, until the purified spirit was released. Intense as was the agony of being thus suddenly called to part with so precious a treasure, without even a word of recognition,—there was solace in the blessed assurance, that in redeeming love and mercy, he was removed from the cares, disappointments and responsibilities attendant on his chosen vocation in this life, to appear before the throne of God, and (with enlarged and it may be ever increasing powers) to serve Him day and night in His temple.

JOHN THOMPSON, 67 7 7 mo. 1870
Morland in Westmoreland.

R

JOHN TOULMIN, 80 14 9 mo. 1870
    Preston, Lancashire.

GEORGE TOWNSON, 5½ 31 3 mo. 1870
    Nether Kellett, Yealand. Son of William and
    Mary Townson.

JAMES TRIPLOW, 36 4 2 mo. 1870
    Chatteris.

ELIZABETH TULLY, 72 18 6 mo. 1870
    Cootehill, County Cavan.

MARGARET UNTHANK, 56 5 11 mo. 1870
    Limerick. Wife of Gabriel Fisher Unthank.

This Friend died at the house of her brother-in-law, Ritson Southall of Elm Villa, Kingston Hill, Surrey. Her end was peace.

SARAH WADHAM, 62 6 6 mo. 1870
    Ackworth, near Pontefract.

This Friend, better known to many by her maiden name as Sarah Madox, spent nearly one half of her life in the service of Ackworth School: holding first the situation of nurse, and afterwards of housekeeper, to that large establishment. She was distinguished by energy, activity, and conscientiousness in the discharge of her responsible duties. Having entered the Society of Friends by convincement, she retained a steady adherence to the religious views she had thus embraced: and though taking no conspicuous place in the

Society, it is believed her mind was often exercised in secret for its true prosperity. She was a visitor of the poor and of the sick : and her judgment and experience in cases of illness were valued by many.

She only retired from active life on her marriage, two years previous to her decease. Of later years she had been afflicted with deafness, which the advice of a London physician failed to relieve : and in addition to this increasing infirmity, during the winter of 1868-9 her general health gave way. Her last illness was brief, she being confined to her room not many days. The few who visited her during its continuance, testify to her settled faith and hope in Christ. She looked forward to the approaching General Meeting, and was interested in the expected visit of Sarah Smiley : and sometimes, in the mental rambling occasioned by her disease, was perplexed with the uprising of former anxieties to have all things ready : but in more lucid moments said resignedly, "I shall be carried to my resting place before then." She also said, "she longed to be gone, but must patiently wait and quietly hope to the end." On being asked one morning how she was ? she replied, "I am fast hastening to Jesus."

SARAH WAKEFORD,   60 14   2 mo. 1870
  Brighton.

The Friend whose name we here record was the daughter of a respectable farm labourer, and was born at Denton in the County of Sussex. At the age of thirteen, she entered into service in the family of the late John Hilton of Brighton, and remained a faithful and much attached domestic in the same family till her death, a period of nearly half a century. She was brought up in attendance on the worship of the Established Church, and became decidedly religious when a young woman. She afterwards joined in membership with an Independent Congregation in Brighton, and for many years was a regular attender at their chapel, until the minister, whose Gospel labours she highly valued, left the town. After this she wandered about, attending successively for a time three different chapels; but not finding that edification she sought after, at last found comfort in uniting herself with the Society of Friends. She was punctual and regular in her attendance of meetings, both on First-day and in the week. The writings of Friends had long been a part of her religious reading; and she was diligent in her study of the Holy Scriptures. She read much in the Bible and other books to the children of the family, and manifested a desire for their spiritual welfare; generally having a word in season to say to them. Though by no means parsimonious, and though always ready to help in need, she left to her friends £200 out of her earnings. But her conduct evinced that she felt the value and truth of Solomon's declaration: " Wisdom is the principal thing: therefore get wisdom; and with all thy getting, get understanding." We have nothing striking to record of her last hours: but there is good ground for believing that her end was peace.

MARTHA ANN WALDUCK,   84 19 5 mo. 1870
   Cheltenham.

JOHN WALKER, Q.C.,   75 6 11 mo. 1869
   Little Heath, Potter's Bar, near Barnet.

SPENCE WALKER,   67 19 7 mo. 1870
   Birstwith, near Ripley, Yorkshire.

DAVID WALTON, *Sheffield.*   78 29 10 mo. 1869

SAMUEL MANLY WATSON,   23 3 5 mo. 1870
   Rathmines, Dublin. Son of John Watson.

MARION WEBB, *Dublin.*   18½ 20 10 mo. 1869
   Daughter of Thomas and Mary Webb.

   During the last six months of the life of this dear young person, while her body and strength were gradually declining, her spirit was becoming purified, and perfectly willing to leave this life and all its temporal enjoyments, the refinements, beauties, and friendships of which she nevertheless loved: and she was enabled with joy to resign her will to that of her Heavenly Father.

A beautiful serenity surrounded her in this period of decline. Her eyes grew brighter, and the colour remained in her face with a peaceful, happy expression. Most of the summer she was able to sit out in a garden, at work or reading; and surrounded with flowers, in which she delighted, and which were constantly sent her as presents from her friends. She appeared in a sweet and happy state of mind, never complaining, even when so weak as not to be able to turn herself. She did not seem weary, never was restless, but just in a cheerful voice asked to have any change made, and to the last enjoyed visits from her acquaintances.

She gave a cheerful assent to the suggestion that she might not recover, with an acknowledgment of peace in the prospect of the life to come. But her parents were exceedingly anxious for some more distinct evidence, that her Saviour had indeed drawn her to Himself. She was one who shrank from expressing anything she did not fully feel. One morning a few days before her death, and the last day she was up, some remarks were made to her on this important subject, but she felt too weak to reply. During the day however, as she lay on the sofa, scarcely able to hold a pencil, she wrote in a trembling and scarcely legible hand as follows : *"For Papa. My Heavenly Father has been very merciful to me—I love Him—I am thankful—I trust in Him—"* adding her intention to write more the following day, but her weakness increased so much she was not able.

The last passage of Scripture she wished to have read to her was the xiv. chapter of John, which speaks of the mansions prepared by the Lord Jesus for His followers, that He is the way, the truth, and the life, and manifests Himself to those who love Him. Her near relatives, while affectionately cherishing her memory, rejoice in believing that she is set free from the trials and the evil of this world, and removed to a home of purity and truth and eternal bliss.

WILLIAM HENRY WEBB, 32 28 5 mo. 1870
Dublin. Son of William and Maria Webb.

RICHARD WEBSTER, 50 2 3 mo. 1870
Blackburn.

WILLIAM WELLS, 64 31 8 mo. 1869
Stoke Newington.

HAROLD ARTHUR WESTLAKE, 4¼ 6 6 mo. 1870
Southampton. Son of William Colson Westlake.

RACHEL WHEATLEY, *York,* 70 13 11 mo. 1869

SAMUEL WHITE WHITE,   56 20 11 mo. 1869
    Lyncombe, near Bath.

ELIZABETH WHITE,   36   4   3 mo. 1870
    Waterford. Died at Nice. Wife of Henry
    White.

HANNAH WHITEHEAD,   89 26 10 mo. 1869
    Chelmsford. Daughter of William Marriage
    Whitehead, late of Bicleigh, near Maldon.

CHARLES HENRY WHITLOW, 35 13   7 mo. 1870
    Wakefield.

ANN WIGHAM,   65   2   1 mo. 1870
    Coanwood. Widow of Thomas Wigham.

MARY WIGHAM, *Doncaster.* 69   5   5 mo. 1870

MARY WIGHAM, *Carlisle.* 70 31   7 mo. 1870
    Of this dear Friend it may be truly said, she
    had, in no ordinary degree, " the ornament of
    a meek and quiet spirit : " and her friends
    cannot but entertain on her account the " hope
    full of immortality," that through the redemp-
    tion that is in Christ Jesus, she has been
    received into His presence with exceeding joy.

MARY EDITH WILSON,   2 12   1 mo. 1870
    Broughton, Manchester. Daughter of Thomas
    Silk and Hannah Wilson.

MARY WOOD, *Liverpool.* 72 17   2 mo. 1870
    An Elder. Wife of William Wood.

SARAH WOOD,   64   3   9 mo. 1870
    Ackworth, near Pontefract.

MARY ISABEL WORSDELL, 4 27 9 mo. 1870
Altoona, Pennsylvania. Died at Yealand in
Lancashire. Daughter of Thomas William and
Mary Ann Worsdell.

MATILDA DE PRICE WRIGHT, 75 24 2 mo. 1870
Mansfield. Widow of John Wright of Lough-
borough.

THOMAS WRIGHT, *Dublin.* 24 4 3 mo. 1870
Son of Eliza and the late Thomas Wright.

JOSEPH WRIGHT, *Derby.* 50 14 4 mo. 1870

SARAH URSULA WYCHERLEY, 22 5 7 mo. 1870
Banbury. Daughter of James and Sarah
Wycherley.

———

INFANTS whose Names are not Inserted.

Under one month	Boys 6 ...	Girls 0
From one to three months...	do. 8 ...	do. 8
From three to six months...	do. 8 ...	do. 8
From six to twelve months	do. 2 ...	do. 7

N.B. It has been suggested to the Editor, to
give the *death-rate per* 1000 on the period included
in our Obituary. We believe the following may be
taken as a near approximation: from the returns
made to the Yearly Meeting. Members in Great
Britain 13,955, in Ireland 2902: total 16,857:—
deaths recorded 319, being 18·92 per 1000 *on a period
of twelve months.* Last year it was 21·48 per 1000.

TABLE.

Shewing the Deaths, at different Ages, in the Society of Friends, in Great Britain and Ireland, during the Years 1867—68, 1868—69, and 1869—70.

AGE.	YEAR 1867—68.			YEAR 1868—69.			YEAR 1869—70.		
	Male.	Female.	Total.	Male.	Female.	Total.	Male.	Female.	Total.
Under 1 year*	9	17	26	20	9	29	14	13	27
Under 5 years	18	23	41	39	21	60	26	26	52
From 5 to 10 years ..	3	1	4	2	5	7	4	0	4
„ 10 to 15 „ ..	2	1	3	5	4	9	1	1	2
„ 15 to 20 „ ..	2	6	8	5	4	9	3	5	8
„ 20 to 30 „ ..	7	14	21	11	8	19	13	11	24
„ 30 to 40 „ ..	4	13	17	8	13	21	10	7	17
„ 40 to 50 „ ..	6	8	14	5	8	13	8	9	17
„ 50 to 60 „ ..	14	15	29	19	22	41	15	17	32
„ 60 to 70 „ ..	22	43	65	29	30	59	23	31	54
„ 70 to 80 „ ..	37	54	91	30	48	78	30	34	64
„ 80 to 90 „ ..	10	35	45	14	23	37	19	22	41
„ 90 to 100 „ ..	0	4	4	2	6	8	0	4	4
All ages	125	217	342	169	192	361	152	167	319

*The numbers in this series are included in the next, "under 5 years."

Average age in 1867—68, .. 55 years, 6 months, and 8 days.
Average age in 1868—69, .. 50 years, 9 months, and 5 days.
Average age in 1869—70, .. 51 years, and 17 days.

JOSIAH FORSTER,

Aged 88.

"In labours more abundant."

In attempting a notice, however imperfect, of the lengthened life and services of one so widely known and so generally beloved as Josiah Forster, we cannot more appropriately express our feelings, than in words written many years ago by our late dear friend himself, upon hearing of the increasing illness of Stephen Grellet. "It affects me to think of the declining health of many whom I have long loved and honoured in the Church; to think of those of a former generation, and to be ready to say, where are their successors? But I know it is unprofitable, and even wrong, to indulge in these thoughts. I am often checked by the consideration, that He who so loved the world as to give Himself for the world, loveth His own cause infinitely better than mortals can. He has all power in Heaven and on earth. To Him, then, let us seek to commit the Church and our own souls, praying that we may be found filling that rank which He appoints for us, and be preserved faithful to the end."

Josiah Forster was born at Tottenham on the 2nd of the Seventh month, 1782. He was the eldest of eleven children, of whom nine grew up to mature age. His parents, William and Elizabeth Forster, were valued members of our Religious Society, and anxiously concerned to train up their children in the fear and love of their Heavenly Father.

" Our dear brother," writes one of his sisters, " gave proof, when quite a boy, of an intelligent mind, and a facility for acquiring foreign languages. He was sent at an early age, as a day scholar, to the school established about the year 1750 by our grandfather, and never left the paternal home except for short periods, until he entered upon his engagements at Southgate. In his disposition he was lively and affectionate, but I think the play-ground was never so attractive to him as to his brother William, who was next in age to him ; and to whom, notwithstanding the difference of their dispositions, he was very closely attached."

He early gave a preference for the occupation of a teacher ; and was engaged for some years as an assistant in his uncle Thomas Coar's school at Tottenham ; during which period, he was in the habit of attending in London the lectures of Dr. Friend and Dr. Walker, and other eminent professors. About the year 1805, he opened a boarding school at Southgate, near Winchmore Hill, for the sons of the wealthier members of our Religious Society, which he continued to carry on there and afterwards at Tottenham, until the year 1826. His teaching was of a superior order. His kindliness of disposition may have occasionally led to an undue relaxation of discipline; but if the labours of a teacher are to be judged by the general result, Josiah Forster had the privilege of seeing not a few of his pupils, many of whom he survived, become under the Divine blessing useful and honourable men, and some of them distinguished ornaments in both civil and religious society.

Having early submitted to the yoke of Christ, his active and intelligent mind appeared peculiarly susceptible to the work of Divine grace, and he derived much profit from intercourse with many highly.esteemed Friends of that day, amongst whom he would often refer to David Barclay, (the grandson of Robert Barclay, the author of the *Apology*,) and especially to Joseph Gurney Bevan and the late Mary Stacey, in whom, as he describes them, " bright mental endowments," were happily blended with large " Christian experience." Their counsel and

s

example, their judicious care, their confidence
and friendship, were greatly blessed to him.
Nor should another dear and valued friend, who
like Joseph Gurney Bevan has passed away
without any direct descendants, be forgotten in
this connexion. " With what esteem do I think
of John Eliot," to quote a memorandum written
in his 88th year, " whose sterling, retiring
character, whose sound judgment and experience
I love to call to mind." Of J. G. Bevan and
John Eliot, as well as of Lindley Murray, Richard
Reynolds, William Grover, and Sarah Hustler,
and many others, with whom he became at a
later period more or less associated in Christian
friendship, Josiah Forster has left loving and
instructive memorials in the eleventh part of
"Piety Promoted," a book, the perusal of which
we would warmly recommend to our youthful
readers.

In the year 1808, he was united in marriage
to Rachel, the daughter of John Wilson of Kendal,
who was the only son of Isaac and Rachel Wilson
of that place ; a union which continued to the close
of his life, and was crowned by a large measure
of the blessing of the Lord.

He was in his 29th year when he first
became a member of the " Meeting for Suffer-

ings;" and he was appointed a few years later to the station of Elder. This may not be the place to enlarge upon his manifold labours in connexion with these and other responsible appointments, as well as in other ways for the good of his fellow-members in religious profession. His frequent visits to the various meetings of Friends in Great Britain and Ireland and on the Continent of Europe,—and on two separate occasions in the United States in his 64th and 72nd years,—his "care for all the churches" under our name through a long course of years,—are well known, and cannot soon be forgotten.

But it may not be equally remembered, that besides the important services which he was accustomed to render in connection with more public documents, he printed in his own name several books and small treatises, which from their unadorned piety and sterling worth may still be read with profit. Amongst these may be noticed, " A Memoir of Joseph Gurney Bevan ;" " A Memoir of William Grover, with Selections from his Letters ;" a volume of " Biographical Notices of Deceased Friends," issued as the eleventh part of " Piety Promoted ;" a small volume containing " An Account of the Christian Principles of Friends," which is interesting as the last volume that obtained the sanction of the " Morning Meeting;" " Letters to Young Friends;" " An Address to Friends in America," and several other smaller papers.

His early interest in the cause of education never flagged. He was one of the founders of the Grove House School at Tottenham, established in 1828 to supply the want occasioned by his own retirement; and, within a few days of his decease, he took his wonted part in attending the Committee of Management, and at the close spent a considerable time in what proved a final interview with the Principal. From 1837 to 1845 he was a working member of the Friends' Educational Society. Our public schools long claimed a large share of his time and attention. He was one of the early advocates, and to the last the faithful supporter, of the cause of Scriptural instruction. His connexion with Ackworth School extended over the long period of forty years, and was the means of affording him opportunities which he highly prized, and much personal communication with those whom he loved. " How pleasant," he writes, " was my intercourse with Samuel Tuke and Joseph Rowntree, with Thomas Pumphrey and my valued cousin Robert Jowitt, on the interests of Ackworth School! an institution which I have again and again visited in years past."

As a young man, Josiah Forster had listened with interest to the proceedings of the Yearly Meeting in 1802 in the case of Hannah Barnard. As clerk of the Yearly Meeting in 1829, he signed the memorable declaration issued in that year, on the occasion of the Hicksite Secession in America. And the prominent part which he was called to take in an important case between the years 1812 and 1814, seems to justify and require more than a merely passing allusion.

A Friend belonging to Ratcliff Monthly Meeting, a man of intelligence and influence, though not in any official station, had become a member of the Unitarian Book Society, and had "distributed papers calling in question the omnipotence of our Lord and Saviour Jesus Christ, and the propriety of applying to Him in secret supplication." On these grounds he was disowned by his Monthly Meeting in the year 1812, and this decision was afterwards confirmed by the Quarterly Meeting of London and Middlesex. The Friend then appealed to the Yearly Meeting of 1814, and Luke Howard, John Eliot, Josiah Forster, and William Allen were, with another Friend, appointed Respondents in behalf of the Quarterly

Meeting. The Committee of Appeal, twenty-seven in number, to whom it was in the first instance referred by the Yearly Meeting, unanimously re-affirmed the judgment; our late friend Jonathan Hutchinson expressing his concurrence in a few pointed words: " I do not know what may have been the experience of my brethren, but for myself I can truly say, that without Christ I should be of all men most miserable."

The case was then brought for final determination before the Yearly Meeting at large : and after an opening address from the appellant, the statement of the respondents was read to the Yearly Meeting by Josiah Forster. Its closing sentences are to the following effect. " The appellant has repeatedly alleged, that he never denied the Eternal Divinity of that Power, which dwelt in and acted by or through the Man Christ Jesus. But in this we can discover no acknowledgment of the Divinity of our Lord, which would imply that He differs, (except in the degree or measure of the power conferred,) from eminently gifted servants, from the Prophets, and the Apostles. How remote from this is the manner in which our ancient Friends, the instruments under Providence in gathering and establishing our Society, understood those passages in Scripture, which speak of Christ as the Word which was in the beginning with God, and was God;—which make mention of the glory that He had with the Father before the world was; of the creation by Him of all things that are in heaven and that are in earth, visible and invisible;—which affirm that all things were created by Him and for Him, that He is before all things, and that by Him all things consist;—which speak of His coming down from heaven;—of His being in the form of God, thinking it not robbery to be equal with God, yet making Himself of no reputation, and taking on Him the form of a servant;—which designate Him as the Son, whom God hath appointed heir of all things, by whom also He made the worlds;—who, being the brightness of His glory, and the express image of His person (or substance,) and upholding all things by the word of His power, when He had by Himself purged our sins, sat down on the right hand of the Majesty on high,—as the Lamb that was slain, to whom, jointly with Him that sitteth on the throne, is ascribed blessing and honour, and glory, and power, for ever and ever! We may," continued the respondents, " in conclusion, express our firm persuasion, that it will appear clear to the Yearly Meeting, that the

Appellant has imbibed, and aided in propagating, opinions contrary to those of our Society; and that having made no concession of being in error, it became the Monthly Meeting, on this occasion of vital importance in regard to our Christian faith, to testify its disunity with him as a member of our Society; and that it was incumbent on the Quarterly Meeting to confirm such judgment."

After a reply from the Appellant the parties withdrew; and the subsequent proceedings cannot be better described than in the words of an eye-witness: — "A solemn silence overspread the whole meeting, and continued for a considerable time uninterrupted. At length William Grover arose. In a single expressive sentence, he pronounced his judgment against the Appellant. After him our elder Friends rose one after another, all with the same sentiment; then Friends in the middle stages of life, and then the young. I never heard so many, or so various Friends speak to any point in our Annual Assembly; and blessed be the name of Him whom alone we acknowledge to be our Saviour and our Head, all were of one accord."* The final judgment of the Yearly Meeting was in the following terms:—" This meeting having deliber-

* See J. J. Gurney's Memoirs, Vol. 1.

ately considered the case of [the appellant] on his appeal from the Quarterly Meeting of London and Middlesex,—also the report of the Committee of this meeting appointed to hear and judge of the said appeal,—is (with much unanimity) of the judgment, that the report of the said Committee should be confirmed; and it is hereby confirmed accordingly." There are Friends now living upon whom the proceedings of that Yearly Meeting made a deep and lasting impression, and who well remember the important service which Josiah Forster was enabled to render as one of the respondents.

But the labours of our dear Friend were not limited to his own Religious Society. He joined the Anti-Slavery Society at an early period, and was for many years one of the most zealous and active members of the Committee. He accompanied his brother William Forster in the year 1845, as a deputation to present the appeal of the Yearly Meeting against Slavery, to the Governments of Prussia and Austria, and was with him on his last journey for this object in the United States in 1853-54.

Another object in which he was deeply interested was the great and important work of the British and Foreign Bible Society. Elected on the Committee in 1826, he continued a member until his decease, with the exception of three years (1840, 1846, and 1854,) during which he was engaged in the fulfilment of important missions abroad, under appointment of our Yearly Meeting.* Steadfast in his adherence to the original basis of that Society,— when a resolution was passed in the year 1857, that all the meetings of the Committee should be opened with prayer, he entered a calm but firm protest against the proceeding; and subsequently wrote a letter to his fellow-members of the Committee explanatory of his views : in which, while clearing setting forth the objection of Friends "to any arrangement for the offering of words at stated times of man's appointment," he carefully guards against the common misconception of their views, as to the importance and necessity of the great duty of prayer. "Prayer," he beautifully says, "is the atmosphere in which the Christian breathes, the very element in which he is nourished and strengthened."

Josiah Forster was a bright example of the blessing that rests upon early dedication. He

* It must be recollected, that continuance on the General Committee of the British and Foreign Bible Society is dependent on regularity of attendance.

loved the Lord from his youth. Retiring early from business upon a moderate competency, he was enabled to devote a lengthened life to the cause of Christ and the good of his fellow-men. Simple both in his personal habits, and in his style and manner of living, he was conscientiously liberal according to his means, and loved to encourage generosity in others. They who visited him will remember the kindly welcome, the Christian courtesy,—the conversation, cheerful without frivolity, marked at once by intelligence and love,—the rooms unadorned with pictures, yet with the air of comfort beyond all the tracery of art or affectation.

Whilst his bodily vigour continued, he was in the habit of walking much, and was remarkable for the activity and rapidity of his movements. As he advanced in age he became more infirm, and of latter years his movements were attended with difficulty. But he exerted himself diligently to the last, and often surprised his friends by the regularity of his attendance at Meetings and Committees; and by his many calls of sympathy and love. Faithful and sincere in his friendships, he was a true sympathizer in distress and sorrow; and from his long experience, was enabled feelingly to enter into the difficulties and trials of life under

many of its varied aspects. His Christianity led
him to take a very humble view of himself, and
to make large allowance for the infirmities of
others. He hated detraction. If he reproved
the fault of a brother, it was with a simplicity
and tenderness, that carried home the conviction
that the reproof was not without cause. His
love was unchilled by age. Indeed it seemed to
flow on in a stream that was ever widening and
deepening with his increasing years. An
extensive correspondence continued to the last
to give evidence of his lively concern, for the
good of others in all parts of the world. His
American Friends especially enjoyed a large
share of his affectionate regard, and the last
efforts of his pen on the very day in which he
was taken sick, were devoted to some whom
he had long loved in that land.

His quickness of perception, was combined
with a sagacity which enabled him to mark and to
appreciate passing events, and the varying currents
of opinion, and to discern the exigencies of the
present day, to an extent remarkable in one who
retained to the last so clear a recollection, and so
high an estimate, of the *past*. Firmly attached,
from conviction, to the distinguishing principles
of our Religious Society, he loved them in their

essential connexion with fundamental Christian truth. His membership amongst Friends was to him a manifestation of his allegiance to Christ, in whom he rejoiced to feel that he had sweet communion with the universal Church of the redeemed. Of these and other features of his character, his private memoranda afford ample illustration. The limits of a notice like the present do not allow room for more than the following selections :—

1831, Seventh mo., 31st. (On recovering from what appeared a slight threatening of paralysis). "I have been confined at home for several days, from an affection which for a time seemed of a serious character. I wish, with humble reverent gratitude, to record the calmness with which I have been favoured to bear this unexpected interruption to my health. I deserved not this help at the merciful hand of our Heavenly Father. My beloved wife, and myself, have been separately and unitedly enabled to return thanks for the Lord's unmerited blessing. May there be in me increased devotedness to the service of our Lord and Saviour!" Evening.—"And now, Lord, what wait I for? my hope is in Thee. All my springs are in Thee. God is the strength of my heart, and my portion for ever. May I daily

T

press after the experience of the truth of these precious words!"

1839, Second mo., 14th. "In the prospect of travelling on the Continent with Elizabeth Fry, the prayer arises that in our going forth we may daily seek unto God, as our helper, guide and support. May there be an humble fervent exercise for the advancement of vital godliness, true spirituality, a growth in grace, and a coming in faith unto Jesus, on the part of those whom we visit! May there be no compromise of what I believe to be Christian principle and practice!"

Second mo., 20th, 1840. "I have with thankfulness to say, that having on Third-day morning spoken amiss in a feeling of impatience, it has brought with it sorrow, and that conviction for sin, which I prize. Having confessed my sin unto the Lord, and sought forgiveness, I have felt a sense of His love, and believe that I may look unto Him again in faith through Christ. My heart rejoices. May it render me increasingly humble and watchful! These humiliations teach me how weak I am. I am not to *presume* on the continuance of Divine mercy and love, but to strive against the first buddings of evil, and earnestly to betake myself to prayer."

Eighth month, 15th, 1840. At Kendal, after

attending the funeral of a brother-in-law.—"I had a walk yesterday afternoon to Benson-knot, a high hill two or three miles distant, commanding a view of the valley and of the distant mountains. A lively, sweet reflection arose in connection with those passages in the Revelation, 'They shall hunger no more, neither thirst any more. The city had no need of the sun, neither of the moon to shine in it, for the glory of the Lord did lighten it, and the Lamb is the light thereof.' I thought of my beloved brother, as among those who worship and praise continually before the throne: the remembrance of these thoughts is precious to-day. It was soon cloudy and rainy—an emblem of our pilgrimage in this life. There is sunshine, and there is the valley of the shadow of death, but afterwards come eternal peace and light. O! the unspeakable goodness of God in Christ Jesus!"

Third month, 26th, 1843. "The views of Friends are to me of unspeakable importance. They should be upheld both practically and by well-qualified writers, men who through experience can testify of the blessedness of waiting upon God. They are no speculative, mystical views. Founded in a sense of the corruption of the human heart, and of the infinite wisdom and love of God in sending His Son into the world to die for our sins, and to be the ever present ruler and leader of His people,—they bring to a practical and entire submission to Him as King and Lord, exercising His authority in the power of His Spirit, enabling His followers to keep His precepts, and in all things to be His servants; in the blessed assurance that they who keep the faith, shall be presented by Christ before the presence of His Father with exceeding joy."

Fourth month, 5th, 1848. "I went yesterday with Samuel Gurney to the burial of Guizot's mother, a worthy Christian; in her old age she followed him in his flight to England. Duchatel and Gabriel Delessert were there; very few beside. It is a striking proof of the instability of human power, thus to see men, high in authority a short time since, exiles in this land, suddenly despoiled of all their influence. I called on Guizot on Second-day; he is brought down. I disapprove of his doings about Tahiti, his want of firmness in the abolition of slavery, of his countenancing the Spanish marriages, and of the vexatious treatment of serious, awakened, religious congregations in France. But he has often been kind to me in that country, and I feel for him now."

Seventh month, 20th, 1854. "How varied are the circumstances of the true believers in the Lord

Jesus! The true members of His Church are to be found among Episcopalians, Presbyterians, Methodists, Baptists, Independents, Friends, and others. They may not know each other, but they are all known to the blessed Head of the Church. They differ from one another in their views of discipline, and on some points of doctrine, but they all appeal to Holy Scripture as the divinely authorized record of the way of life and salvation. How incumbent upon them it is to love one another, as brethren in Christ! And this they can do, whilst everyone is fully persuaded in his own mind of that, to which it is right for him to adhere."

1855, Ninth mo., 13th. "To none, I believe, are the Holy Scriptures so truly precious, as to him who is the furthest advanced in the Christian course; to him they are an exhaustless mine of wealth. The freshness with which they are brought home to him, is a delightful confirmation that they truly come from God. But there is a state of mind in which some may think, that every act of the religious man is to be measured or determined by some specific passage of Scripture. Is there not in that state a danger of mistaking the means for the end? The Scriptures are an invaluable treasure, in that they are the appointed means of making known to mankind the glorious truths which they contain. But it is the *Spirit of God* which can alone change the evil heart of man. It is *Christ* who is the light of the world—the life of man. And is it not to be feared that with some professors of faith in Christ, there is too much of a resting in the knowledge of Scriptural truths, rather than an earnestness of soul to know the heart cleansed of every defilement, by the application of them through the power of the Spirit."

Fourth mo., 28th, 1865. "The sudden death, on this day two weeks, of the President of the United States, by the hand of an assassin, has greatly distressed me. For a few hours I could not bring the mind to a simple acquiescence with the will of the Most High, in permitting this solemn event. In His unmerited kindness and pity, I am much easier to-day."

Sixth mo., 4th, 1865. "I think of Friends in America with warm desires now that peace is restored in the land, that their daily walk may not only give evidence of their gratitude to the Lord for this great blessing, but that their lives and conversation may prove the sincerity of their thanksgiving and of their faith in Him."

Recounting His many mercies, he writes under date Ninth mo., 3rd, 1864. "How great has been my enjoyment of the kindness, the confidence, and the society of many, who have sought to be devoted servants of their Saviour and Redeemer! What a large amount of health has been my portion! I have been tempted neither with riches nor with poverty. I have had the privilege of most kind and watchful and tender Christian parents; not taken from me in my youth, but living to a good old age, and dying in the faith and hope of the Gospel. A most precious, loving, faithful wife, brothers and sisters who have loved me, and been loved by me, and who have been treated by others with respect and honour. Well may I say, Thou hast, O Lord, crowned me with loving kindness and tender mercies! In the multitude of my thoughts within me, ought Thy comforts to delight my soul."

A serious illness which confined him to the house for many weeks in the beginning of 1870, greatly impaired his strength, and left effects from which he never entirely recovered. As the spring advanced he was able to resume his usual occupations, and his friends encouraged the hope that he would be yet spared to them a little longer. He was able to take his accustomed part in most of the deliberations of the last Yearly Meeting in London, and to attend to the engagements of several

important Committees. On the 15th of the Sixth
month he accompanied a deputation of the Anti-
Slavery Society to Lord Clarendon, on the subject
of the continuance of Slavery in Cuba. The aged
Christian and the veteran statesman met for the
last time; in less than two weeks from that interview, both finished their earthly course on the
morning of the same day. How much have they
each been mercifully spared! How little could
either of them foresee the violent convulsion, that
was so soon to spread ruin and desolation over the
fairest countries of Europe, and to bring distress
and anguish to thousands of homes! " It is touching to think," writes a correspondent, " that it is
scarcely a fortnight since I went with the Anti-
Slavery Society's deputation to Lord Clarendon.
Our dear aged friend would go up all those long
stairs into the new Foreign Office; I helped him
up step by step. Lord Clarendon shook hands
with him warmly, and said there were few who
had worked longer in the Anti-Slavery cause, than
Josiah Forster and himself. At the end of the
interview, Josiah Forster thanked Lord Clarendon
for the part he had always taken, in upholding
England's testimony against slavery; and having
succeeded thus far, he trusted that now, at the
verge of general success, England's influence

would be steadily used in the utter extinction of this baleful traffic throughout the world. At the close of the interview, I helped him part of the way down stairs, leaving him as he wished to call at the Privy Council to see his nephew, William Edward."

On the 20th he was, for the last time, at the meeting of the Committee of the British and Foreign Bible Society. A question in which he felt a very lively concern, and which had caused him some anxiety, was about to be discussed. He availed himself of the permission of the chairman, to make the observations he had to offer, without rising from his seat. "They were pervaded," say the Committee in a memorial subsequently published, "by that tone of holy gratitude and love so familiar to the Committee; and he expressed his thankfulness that a result had been obtained in connection with the work of the Society, so entirely in unison with his own present wishes and prayers."

On the following Fourth-day, the 22nd, a small sub-committee, in connection with the business of the Yearly Meeting, met at his house. The interview proved almost too much for his strength, but on the following morning he attended the Mid-week Meeting as usual; and the next day, Sixth-day, the 24th, he wrote three letters to America. This last effort exhausted him, and it was with difficulty that he was helped to his chamber. Erysipelas supervened; his little remaining strength rapidly failed : and early on Second-day morning, the 27th of the Sixth month, he quietly breathed his last. The interment took place at Winchmore Hill, on the 2nd of the Seventh month, the day on which he would have completed his 88th year. It was largely attended by his friends from various parts, including a deputation from the Committee of the British and Foreign Bible Society.

Born a few months previously to the recognition by this country of the Independence of the United States, and seven years before the breaking out of the great French Revolution, the recollections of his early manhood were associated with the awful ravages of war on the European Continent under the First Napoleon; and amidst the sanguinary conflicts of more recent times, his mind seemed almost instinctively to recur to the deep impressions left upon it, by the cruelties of such generals as Massena and Suwarrow,—to the " burning of Moscow, and to the dreadful hardships of the war in Saxony, and other neighbouring countries, in the years 1812 and 1813."

Though not yet nine years old at the decease of
John Wesley, he was for upwards of fifty years
the cotemporary of Rowland Hill and of William
Wilberforce, and for many years the friend and
associate of Thomas Clarkson, Zachary Macaulay,
and others no less earnest in the struggle against
slavery. Though not himself present at the
formation of the British and Foreign Bible
Society, he would often recur with pleasure to
his distinct recollection of it, and as a young
man was well acquainted with the three Friends
who formed part of the original Committee, Wilson
Birkbeck, the brother-in-law of his early friend
Joseph Gurney Bevan, — Robert Howard, the
father of Luke Howard, — and Joseph Smith,
whose wife was the sister of his valued friend
Mary Stacey. Elder by several years than the
late Sir Thomas Fowell Buxton and Joseph John
Gurney, he esteemed his intercourse with them,
and with William Allen, Joseph Sturge, Peter
Bedford, and others like-minded, one of his greatest privileges. Josiah Forster was thus one of
the few remaining links, which united the present
with a former generation. He " rests from his
labours ;" but the recollection of his humility, his
faith, his loving spirit, his active zeal, his firmness
in upholding the truth, his life-long dedication to

the cause of his Lord and Master, will live in the hearts of many as a precious memorial. Let it be accepted as a testimony, not to him, but to the power of that redeeming grace, which continues from age to age the one unfailing sufficiency of the children of God; and may all who have known and loved him, or who may hereafter hear or read of him, be impressed as deeply as he was, under the teaching of the same Spirit, with the great and indispensible lesson to which, were he still amongst us, he could point as the great lesson which he had been taught in his lengthened life.

"I write it reverently and thankfully," (such are his words in his 'Note Book,' under date Sixth mo. 29th, 1856), "that I have nothing whatever to look to, but the full and free mercy of God in Christ washing away my sins in His most precious blood. It is with a heart overflowing with gratitude, that I desire to acknowledge, at this hour, that I confide in that great salvation, and wholly commit myself unto my Father in Heaven, in and through the Lord Jesus and the Holy Spirit—one God, blessed for ever."

APPENDIX.

ELIZA LOCKWOOD,

YOUNG IN YEARS, BUT LOVED OF JESUS.

"I LOVE THEM WHO LOVE ME; AND THOSE THAT SEEK
ME EARLY, SHALL FIND ME."—*Prov. viii.*, 17.

There is no doubt that this dear child, born
in an humble sphere of life, and removed by death
at the early age of fourteen, was nevertheless a
scholar in the school of Christ: and following
Him also as the Good Shepherd, was led into the
ways of pleasantness, and into the paths of peace,
and gathered safely into His fold of rest.

She was the third daughter of Thomas and
Ann Lockwood of Highflatts near Huddersfield,
and was born there in the Third month of 1853.
She was always of a quiet and gentle disposition;
and about ten years of age, when the Friends'
First-day School was re-opened, she became from
the first a regular attender. But she was then
only a poor reader: for being one of a large

L

family, she had not gone much to school: yet she was very attentive and persevering, and steadily improved. Even after her parents had removed some three miles from Highflatts, she would come up the hills during the winter mornings in all weathers, and was always ready to repeat her portion of Scripture or hymn. She would learn quite long pieces out of the *British Workman*, or *Band of Hope Review*; and was very ready in answering questions on the Scriptures, evidently taking pleasure in it. Thus she became an example to the other girls, over whom she exercised an influence for good. In her own home, the same influence was felt: and when her brothers had not behaved kindly to her, she subdued them by gentle words,—always loving and affectionate to all.

In the summer of 1866, she went to the Friends' School at Rawden near Leeds, but her stay there was short. Her health began to fail, and she was obliged to leave in the autumn in consequence of a hip disorder, from which she never recovered. Yet during that short period she had won the love and regard of her teachers and schoolfellows, who addressed many affectionate letters to her after she had left, the children nearly all alluding to her kind counsel and persuasion, and styling her their "dear kind little preacher."

Nor did she forget those she had left at home in her father's cottage. Not hearing from them for a good while, she wrote hoping nothing was the matter, but she expressed her trust, "that He who doeth all things well, would keep them safely." A simple letter addressed to her eldest brother, next in age to herself, will show the tenor of her mind.

"My dear Brother,

I hope you are well. Have you begun getting potatoes yet? I see plenty of turnips here, but none like ours at home. I still call it home, and it is a home indeed! a precious home to me, who am away from you. But I will try my best, to do what my father and mother want; and He whose eye is upon me will help me,— and *it is upon you too*, dear John. Remember *that*, when you are tempted to do wrong ;— which I hope you never are. Jesus said, "Suffer little children to come unto me, and forbid them not, for of such is the kingdom of heaven ;" and if we trust in Him, He will also gather us in His bosom, as He did in days of yore, when He died for us ;—*for you too*, dear John ; and you are one of His lambs too, dear brother! 'Blessed are the poor in spirit, for theirs is the kingdom of heaven.' I think of that many a time when tempted to do wrong, and I hope you will also. I also think of you at that sweet spot called home;—and do not forget, dear brother, there is a still sweeter place called heaven, where the good always go. I hope I shall meet you there: it is what I pray for. * * * Give my love to all at home; so farewell, darling John.

I remain your loving sister,

ELIZA LOCKWOOD.

Rawden, 22nd Eighth mo., 1866."

Her illness continued till the middle of the following year, often accompanied with acute pain; but she bore all with remarkable patience: never being heard to express an impatient word, so that her mother could say, " I can't remember ever hearing one murmuring word, though she suffered as few are aware." When racked with pain, she would try to compose herself by repeating the hymns she had learnt: and she would often talk to her little sisters, to be good children and love their Saviour. She was very fond of reading the 139th Psalm.

A few weeks before she died, she said she knew she never would get better, but she felt quite happy in the hope of seeing her dear

Saviour in heaven. When a friend visited her only three days previous to her decease, she said " she was ready to go :—the will of the Lord be done !—and though it was hard to part with those she loved, yet she wanted to go, and be with Jesus."—" I know He loves me, because He has said so :" and then she repeated the passage, " I love them that love Me, and those who seek Me early shall find me,"—and, (she added,) " I *do* love Jesus. O that throng of angels ! when I think of it, it makes me long to go." Speaking of her school fellows, she desired her love to them, " all of them—and tell them I am happy, and going to Jesus, where I hope to meet them every one." She seldom alluded to her sufferings, unless asked, though in great pain : " not my will but Thine be done," was her oft repeated language. Prayer being offered on her account, and the words used, " may Thy rod and Thy staff comfort her," she recalled them again, " Thy rod and Thy staff—they *do* comfort me." Bidding her farewell, the visitor said, " if we do not meet again here, I trust we may in heaven," she replied, " I hope so."

This was her abiding hope. On the morning of her death, she said to her mother, " Don't cry, dear mother, for I believe we shall meet again in heaven." She took an affectionate farewell of her brothers and sisters, kissing them, and bidding them be good children : and on her father taking her in his arms, she said she felt happy, quite happy, and never spoke again ; but went quietly and gradually away. She died on the 7th of Sixth month, 1867 :—young in years, but loved of Jesus :—" of such is the kingdom of heaven."

The late

JOSEPH BENWELL,
of Bristol,

who died in 1864.

Very varied are the dispensations of Providence,—to some are given health and strength, to others wealth and large possessions, to others intellectual riches. While some are called to places of power and influence, others move in an unobserved and very private sphere. Many are the good things that make life pleasant, though to some is measured out the cup of affliction. Whilst few persons are exempt from repeated visitations of sickness in childhood, in youth, in mature age, there are nevertheless individuals who appear to be remarkably free from such trials, and whose years roll along in one continued course of bodily health, till the natural powers suddenly fail, and they also arrive at " the house appointed for all living."

This was largely the experience of the late Joseph Benwell of Bristol, whose protracted life, terminated in 1864, reached back as far as nineteen years into the last century. It was a frequent remark of his, that he was never, in the course of his long life, until a few months before its close, kept one whole day away from business on account of illness. In this he felt he had been privileged beyond many others; and for such a continuance of health and strength he entertained feelings of great thankfulness, his favourite Psalm being the 103rd, " Bless the Lord, O my soul, and all that is within me, bless His holy name. Bless the Lord, O my soul, and forget not all His benefits."

Yet " one event happeneth unto all." After being as usual at business on the 22nd of First month, a little after midnight he was taken suddenly ill with a trying and painful complaint, which confined him to a sick chamber. He looked back on the years that were gone, and dwelt with humbled feelings on the goodness and long-suffering kindness of his Heavenly Father, in sparing him and bearing with him, in all his

wanderings.　In simple rhymes he would say, in
reflecting on the Lord's dealings with him:—

> The course I took was on the brink
> 　Of many a tottering wave,
> And Satan fain would see me sink,
> 　But God was pleased to save.

Or his grateful feelings would find expression
during the night watches as follows:—

> O may it be my chief delight,
> Morning, noon, and solemn night,
> On mercies and on love so great,
> With thankful heart to meditate!

From this first illness he was, however, enabled,
notwithstanding his advanced age, to rally, but
on the 3rd of Fourth month, another attack of a
different character entirely confined him to his
bed.

He was a man of reserved disposition, and
this was especially shown in regard to his religious
feelings: yet his nearest connexions earnestly
wished to hear from him an assurance of the
ground of his hope.　The way for this was opened
by a timely visit from a dear female relative,
whom he used to call his messenger of peace and
comfort.　It was found his heart was giving up
every earthly tie, and ripening for the important
change which was soon to come.　Alluding on

one occasion to the blessing of health, with which he had been so largely favoured, he feelingly remarked,—"and if it had been *wealth*—I should probably have been a castaway !"

He repeatedly spoke of an instructive simile he had met with in his reading, that had much impressed him ; in which a sinner under conviction of his danger is compared to a man struggling in deep waters, plunging and striving in vain by his own efforts to gain the shore, and save himself;—when a rope being thrown to him, he ceases from his own exertions, and seizing the rope is drawn to land, and saved. This he accepted as beautifully illustrative of faith in the Lord Jesus. His religious impressions seem to have been deep, though hidden. He was a regular attender of meetings for worship : but being much afflicted with deafness, he could seldom hear anything that was said in them. He however reverted frequently to one sermon which he had been able to hear, from the late John Pease, on his last visit to their meeting ; which he prized so much that he had written it down from memory.

Probably this difficulty of hearing tended to increase his love of reading. But being one day reminded that he used to be very fond of *Bunyan's*

Pilgrim's Progress, with a remark that in his weak condition he had lost his relish for reading, he said with feeling, "'Prayer all my business, all my pleasure praise:' and when it comes to this, what a favour!" On being asked if he could send a message to a valued friend that he enjoyed peace of soul, he said, "The remembrance of past offences sometimes rises as a cloud before me: but I think I may say, that I have an humble trust; looking for that blessed hope, and the glorious appearing of the great God and our Saviour Jesus Christ."

His illness lasted three months, and was often marked with much tossing and discomfort, and mental rambling: but when seasons of composure returned, they were invariably attended by a quiet confidence, though with a sense of unworthiness:—and although on almost every other subject he would wander incoherently, yet in speaking of his Saviour he was clear and connected.

On Fourth-day previous to his death, he manifested extreme calmness of manner, and broke forth in a sweet and impressive strain on the countless mercies he had received: pressing his hand on his breast, he said, "It is sweet to feel the cords of love drawing me to my

Saviour. I do enjoy it so much. I have had such sweet communion with my dear Heavenly Father this morning : 'tis indeed sweet."—"Oh be pleased," he continued, "to keep us from the power of sin and transgression. What should we do, if we died within the grasp of the wicked one? what *should* we do? O that the meditation of my heart may be acceptable in Thy sight! * * * 'Tis sweet to feel the inflowing of a Saviour's love, sweeter far than the inflowing of ten thousand earthly jewels. How often we feel the predominance of Satan over our hearts! Oh enable us to feel that in Thy strength we can overcome his influence. * * * Be Thou the Shepherd of Thy stray sheep. Oh, I feel like the man struggling in the stream. I must get hold of the rope that is held out to me. I do try to reach it, and I *will* try. More faith! more faith! More faith! full of faith—true sanctification."

It was proposed to read a few verses from the 8th of Romans ; but he said, "I think not now : —'be still, and know that I am God.' I have had a few storms of mental agony, and Satan has pierced me through and through." One of the family saying, "Father, it is now the voice of Jesus in the storm." "Yes," he replied, "saying Peace, be still." A favourite text which he often repeated was, "Goodness and mercy have followed me all the days of my life,—and surely (he would add) He who has borne with me in all my wanderings, will not forsake me in my old age."

His breathing had become very laborious for some days, and painful to witness. The day before he died, he looked up sweetly to his two daughters, and said, " I am praying for you both : a blessing will attend you :" and soon afterwards, though almost inaudible, " Bless the Lord, O my soul." During the day articulation entirely failed ; but he made signs for a slate, and with a tremulous hand asked for portions of scripture to be hung up, as had been done before, that his eye might rest on some precious promise. He appeared to dwell on them again with interest, but nature was exhausted. About nine in the evening his breathing grew calmer. He seemed again to wish to speak ; but though conscious, could not say anything. He watched his beloved wife with great interest, as she gently moved about to relieve his wants : they had been united for six-and-fifty years ! After this, he settled down in sweet composure, and fell asleep in Jesus at one o'clock in the morning, on the 9th of Seventh month 1864, in the 83rd year of his age.

BRADFORD : PRINTED BY JOHN DALE AND CO.

Check Out More Titles From HardPress Classics Series In this collection we are offering thousands of classic and hard to find books. This series spans a vast array of subjects – so you are bound to find something of interest to enjoy reading and learning about.

Subjects:
Architecture
Art
Biography & Autobiography
Body, Mind &Spirit
Children & Young Adult
Dramas
Education
Fiction
History
Language Arts & Disciplines
Law
Literary Collections
Music
Poetry
Psychology
Science
…and many more.

Visit us at www.hardpress.net

CPSIA information can be obtained
at www.ICGtesting.com
Printed in the USA
BVHW040942270819
556819BV00015B/3618/P